Holy Cow! End Times Prophecy Just Got Real

DECODING THE MYSTERIES OF THE LAST DAYS AND THE GOOD NEWS OF JESUS' RETURN

Holy Cow! End Times Prophecy Just Got Real

Decoding the Mysteries of the Last Days and the Good News of Jesus' Return

Annaly Mawire * Jason McKay
Chichi and Tracy Onyekanne

W Publishing Group
An Imprint of Thomas Nelson

Holy Cow! End Times Prophecy Just Got Real

Published in Nashville, Tennessee, by W Publishing, an imprint of Thomas Nelson. W Publishing and Thomas Nelson are registered trademarks of HarperCollins Christian Publishing, Inc.

The authors are represented by Tom Dean, Literary Agent with A Drop of Ink LLC, www.adropofink.pub.

Thomas Nelson titles may be purchased in bulk for educational, business, fund-raising, or sales promotional use. For information, please email SpecialMarkets@ThomasNelson.com.

ISBN 978-1-4003-5346-0 (audiobook)
ISBN 978-1-4003-5345-3 (eBook)
ISBN 978-1-4003-5344-6 (TP)

HarperCollins Publishers, Macken House, 39/40 Mayor Street Upper, Dublin 1, D01 C9W8, Ireland (https://www.harpercollins.com).

Library of Congress Cataloging-in-Publication Data On-file

Printed in the United States of America

26 27 28 29 30 LBC 5 4 3 2 1

Annaly Mawire

To my husband, Stephen, and our children, Harmony and Elijah—my greatest support and inspiration, thank you for walking with me through the wrestle and the wonder. And to you, the reader, who dared to pick this up: May this book ignite fearless faith within you.

Jason McKay

To my sons, Cole and Austin, and to this generation: May these pages awaken you to the reality of God's plan, the urgency of the hour, and the clarity of your calling in these last days.

Chichi Onyekanne

To my wife, Tracy, for standing with me through every late night, every challenging conversation, and every moment of revelation. What an honor it's been. And to the next generation: May you lead with boldness, stand with conviction, and remain faithful even when your faith is tested. The world needs you ready.

Tracy Onyekanne

To my husband, Chichi: I'm in awe that we get to do this together. And to those overwhelmed by the noise of this divided world—the confusion, the fear, and the endless extremes—may these pages lead you beyond opinion and into encounter. I pray they point you not to answers, but to the Answer Himself: Jesus Christ.

CONTENTS

CHAPTER 1

RED THREADS AND RED HEIFERS

An Unlikely Team, an Ancient Search, and God's Perfect Timing

Imagine sitting in a coffee shop with friends when someone casually drops the question, "Do you think we're living in the last days?"

The room suddenly feels heavier. You've seen the headlines: wars, protests, rising tensions in Israel, strange stories about red heifers, and temple talk. You've scrolled through posts with preachers and influencers all saying the same thing: *Jesus is coming soon.* But sitting there with a latte in your hand, you wonder, *What does that actually mean? What will it look like?* How should it affect the way you live tomorrow morning when you clock into work, raise your kids, love your neighbor, or scroll through your feed?

The truth is, as the days go by, there are more and more headlines and voices expressing that we're in "the last days." Last days of what exactly? Life? Earth's existence? The church? That phrase, along with "end times," means so many different things to so many different people. For some, it sparks fear; for others, curiosity; and for many, just confusion. As tensions in the Middle East and globally continue to rise, it's more important than ever that we know and feel confident in the conversation surrounding the end times—not to pinpoint or calculate the exact dates and moments when things will happen, but rather to be confident in our understanding of what God's Word says regarding it all.

This isn't the first time this conversation has sparked, but if you're like us, it feels a little different this time around. There's a sense of urgency in recent years that can't be ignored. People from different denominational backgrounds and upbringings are starting to echo similar things. Something's shifting. There are reports of revival across the nation and the globe. The Bible translation organization illumi*Nations* aims to translate the Bible (New Testament at a minimum) into every known language of the world by 2033.[1] Matthew 24:14 anyone?![2] Speakers, pastors, and evangelists are expressing that Jesus is coming soon and urging the capital *C* church to be ready more than ever. There are wars and rumors of wars. And so much more!

Things are happening around the world, and the body of Christ is taking notice. If someone asked you, "When is Jesus coming back?" how would you respond? (Not the exact moment He's coming back but what Scripture says about His coming back.) Would you have an answer? Would it be an echo of what you've been hearing, or would it be a response that came from Scripture? The Word of God invites us to know and interpret the seasons. And through His Word and the power of His Spirit, we can do just that.

Meet the Team with the Story Behind the Story

Let's back up for a moment. If you're like a lot of people, you may not have done a deep dive on the back of this book to find out who we, the authors, are. How did a group of podcasters land themselves in the middle of something they claim is globally significant? And beyond that, why are there four authors for this book? That seems like a lot!

Believe us, we spent entirely too much time going back and forth with one another and the publishing team about how in the world this would even work. We know the last thing you want is to have to read from four different authors and figure out who's speaking when. Rest assured, that won't be the case for the duration of this book. However, to fully grasp how God orchestrated our paths and how surreal it was to find ourselves on a ranch witnessing a selection process involving potential prophecy-fulfilling red cows (more on that later!), we think it's best to properly introduce ourselves and how we ended up here. We'll be back as one cohesive voice together again after this, but journey with us for a moment. Because here's the thing: When you hear how each of our stories led us to that ranch, and how those personal and collective journeys actually connect to the bigger prophetic picture we're about to unpack, we believe you'll be more in awe of our sovereign God than ever before.

So let's meet the team. Different backgrounds. Different upbringings. Different personalities. But the same God who uniquely placed us in what we believe could be a stage-prepping moment to the return of Christ.

Jason McKay

Ever since I was young, I was captivated by the adventure and mystery in films like *Indiana Jones.* Not simply for the thrill of treasure hunting but for the deeper allure of uncovering ancient secrets. My passion drew me to books, history, and especially prophetic scriptures. There was nothing more exhilarating to me than finding tangible evidence of divine realities hidden within sacred texts. My prayer has always been, "God, I want to be right in the middle of what You're doing in the last days." Little did I know, decades later, I'd find myself living an adventure even more profound than I ever imagined. One that, I would argue, rivals *Indiana Jones.*

My lifelong pursuit of understanding God's kingdom eventually brought me into mentorship with Dr. Robert Mawire, a scholar deeply connected with global prophetic movements, especially concerning Israel. This relationship placed me at the heart of prophetic mysteries that I had only heard and read about. Witnessing the favor and influence he had with leaders around the world was remarkable. I heard testimonies and stories that would be hard to believe if I hadn't physically been in the room.

One day, I received an urgent call from Dr. Mawire. He told me rabbis from Israel would soon be on their way to Texas. They were desperately seeking a spotless red heifer in order to resume temple worship in Jerusalem, something that hadn't happened for nearly two millennia (more on this later!). According to Jewish writing and prominent rabbis, the tenth red heifer would mark the imminent arrival of the Messianic Age.[3] My heart raced with excitement! So many thoughts flooded my mind as I began to understand the significance of the moment.

Out of billions of people alive today, somehow God had

written me into the story in such a way that I was standing at the precipice of what I had prayed for since my youth: to be right in the middle of what He is doing in the last days. In that instant, the scriptures I had studied for years seemed to leap off the page—alive and unfolding before my very eyes.

At the same time, I was fully aware of the weight of what this moment meant for the rabbis. For them, a spotless red heifer represented the doorway back into temple worship. But for me, as a follower of Christ, my heart was fixed on the greater story: the final spotless Lamb of God, who has already made the ultimate sacrifice once and for all. Far from conflicting, these moments stirred hope in me, because I believe even this pursuit will ultimately lead Israel to recognize their true Messiah. Just as the prophet Zechariah declared, "They will look on Me whom they pierced. Yes, they will mourn for Him as one mourns for his only son" (12:10).

The words of Paul in Romans also rang in my heart: "I do not desire, brethren, that you should be ignorant of this mystery . . . that blindness in part has happened to Israel until the fullness of the Gentiles has come in. And so all Israel will be saved, as it is written: 'The Deliverer will come out of Zion, and He will turn away ungodliness from Jacob; for this *is* My covenant with them, when I take away their sins'" (11:25–27). Paul was reminding the church that Israel's story was not over, that a partial hardening was temporary, and that God Himself had promised to send the Deliverer to cleanse His people. The same covenant-keeping God who had preserved them through history would one day open their eyes to the Messiah they had missed.

The thought was overwhelming. Could I truly be witnessing another step toward that promise? The collision of history, prophecy, and destiny swirled together, and all I could do was whisper a prayer of gratitude: *Lord, let me steward this moment well. Let every sign point to You. Let every search ultimately lead back to the Lamb who takes away the sin of the world.*

But soon things would take an unsettling turn. The original rancher scheduled to meet the rabbis abruptly canceled, influenced by his pastor, who warned him that helping in this search would contradict Christ's ultimate sacrifice. (In this book we will emphasize that Jesus was the final sacrifice and atonement for our sins, but we can understand how the search for a spotless red heifer could be confusing if you aren't familiar with the road map of Christ's return.) So we had ourselves a problem: A handful of rabbis were already on their way to the States, but there was no ranch, no herd of Red Angus to examine, and now seemingly no reason for them to make the trip.

Despite the current obstacle, I was excited to share about all that was happening with my dad. He knew how much biblical prophecy meant to me, so I was eager to call him and tell him the latest. When I explained what was happening, his response was nothing short of shocking. "I've got a rancher friend in the Dallas-Fort Worth area who's been raising Red Angus cattle for over twenty years. He's been preparing them for the end times."

I couldn't believe it. I called Dr. Mawire to pass on the news. He responded in disbelief and set up a meeting right away.

On the first urgent visit, Dr. Mawire went alone to the ranch owned by Brian and Ty Davenport, the longtime friends of my dad. Initially hopeful, he quickly became discouraged as each cow they inspected had blemishes or had already been marked or tagged. In a moment of faith, Dr. Mawire suggested they pause and earnestly pray right there in the pasture.

At the moment their prayers were lifted to heaven, something crazy happened. Across the field, a cow went into labor, delivering a calf right before their eyes! Trust me, I know how crazy that sounds, but it was right on par with experiences I had previously had with Dr. Mawire. This newborn calf was entirely red, perfect, and unblemished. A miracle that seemed to clearly have the markings of divine intervention.

Days later, a group gathered with the rabbis at the ranch. As we gathered in the Davenports' living room, I felt an exciting anticipation. One of the rabbis who was leading the red heifer search inexplicably felt compelled to share a fascinating, ancient account of a red heifer selection. With deep reverence, he described how, during preparations for the Second Temple, Jewish priests approached a Gentile diamond dealer in Jerusalem, seeking a special diamond for the high priest's sacred breastplate. Out of respect for his sleeping father, who held the keys to the stones, the dealer postponed their transaction by one day. They tried to offer more money, but this diamond dealer refused. The next day they came back, and the dealer accepted the initial offer. He honored the first price that was set rather than accepting the higher offer they made to expedite the process. Moved by his honorable action, the rabbis prophetically blessed him, declaring his diamonds would adorn the high priest's breastplate and his flocks would produce the rare red heifer needed for temple rituals. And remarkably, it's believed that this prophecy had come true.

An intense silence filled the room as the rabbi finished his story. It felt like my heart was beating outside of my chest as I realized the astonishing connection. Nervously, I glanced toward Byron Stinson, who had orchestrated this meeting, then at Brian

Davenport, who sat stunned. My voice trembled slightly as I softly asked Brian, "Do you want to tell him, or should I?"

Overwhelmed, Brian quietly nodded toward me. Turning to the rabbi, I excitedly revealed, "Rabbi, did you know that Brian, whose cattle you're here to inspect, is also a diamond dealer?"

His eyes widened in disbelief and wonder as the weight of the potential prophetic fulfillment became more real to everyone in the room. Everyone erupted in astonishment and praise. Two stories collided in ways that didn't feel random or coincidental. The last red heifer had been chosen from the herd of a diamond dealer, and—two thousand years later—the next, and possibly final, red heifer might also be selected from the herd of another diamond dealer.

I don't know about you, but how many cattle ranchers do you know who are also diamond dealers? The odds were breathtaking. Although Brian's diamonds weren't being used to make a breastplate for the high priest, the connection felt far too precise to be mere chance!

I couldn't ignore the way that all of the numbers were adding up. Approximately two thousand years had passed since the last red heifer. Jewish tradition foretold that the tenth would signal the beginning of an era of their Messiah's coming, and now, we potentially had the red heifer that could bring this to pass.

My eyes darted around Brian's living room, from the rabbi's astonished expression to Brian's quiet, stunned awe. Every heart in that room was surely aware of the supernatural nature of what was taking place.

In that moment, it felt as if clarity broke through every doubt, every question I'd ever held about my purpose. This couldn't merely be coincidence. Could we really be witnessing

God's arithmetic? Could it be that His fingerprints were this clear upon every detail?

And somehow, impossibly, my life had become part of the equation. The Davenport brothers expressed that a birthing season was happening in a month or so on the ranch. They told us that they would give strict orders to the ranch hands not to tag them. The rabbi began giving specific instructions on what to do when they were born, until they were able to return to examine them.

So much seemed to be happening; it didn't feel real. It was a strange mixture of emotions all at once. I felt overwhelmed in the best possible way, like I was standing in the middle of a living prophecy and history was unfolding around me. My heart pounded with awe and anticipation, but at the same time, my mind struggled to keep up. How could this be real? How could ordinary people like us be caught up in something that sounded like it belonged in the pages of Scripture rather than on a Texas ranch? It felt like stepping into a story bigger than myself; I could sense the fingerprints of God pressing into every detail. This ranch was officially becoming a part of this prophetic process and journey.

A little over a month later I got the call. The calves had been born and the rabbis, even more of them this time, were en route. I felt strongly that I should document this day this time around. I brought along Chichi, a close friend for over a decade, and his wife, Tracy, to capture this extraordinary unfolding prophecy and process. Initially, we believed we were simply recording content for a podcast Chichi and I had planned about biblical prophecy years ago. Little did we know, this footage, along with a few divine relationships, would soon birth something entirely unexpected: our podcast, *Faith and Friction*, vividly capturing the miraculous events surrounding the red heifers.

I felt as if we were standing before an investigative board. You know, the ones you see in crime shows. Each note, photo, and scripture carefully connected by vibrant red threads. The prophecy in Scripture. The red heifers picked out. The land atop the Mount of Olives that the rabbis have secured for the ritual. The temple instruments needed to begin sacrificing again (more on this later!). I found myself on that Red Angus ranch quietly reflecting, speaking directly to God: "Could this ranch really produce the red heifer that prophecy has anticipated for millennia?"

I stepped back thoughtfully, the gravity of the moment pressing heavily on my heart. I considered the intricate timing, the prophetic connections, and the compelling evidence. Each thread undeniably pointed toward something monumental. As I stood there, the realization swept over me that my life's prayer was being answered in the most astounding way. I, Jason McKay, a longtime prophetic explorer, had stepped into an extraordinary adventure that was becoming an integral thread woven into an ancient, ongoing story of divine mystery with prophetic breadcrumbs throughout Scripture. I was ready to see just how this story would unfold.

Tracy Onyekanne

I remember the day like it was yesterday. My husband, Chichi, and I were waiting to see if this red heifer thing was happening. It was only days before Christmas, and we had plans to fly to Pennsylvania to spend the holiday with my family. Even though I was slightly anxious that we would have to change flights and spend less time with my family for, well, cows, I was still up for the adventure. Our cameras were ready to go, and we were excited. We got the confirmation from Jason that the rabbis were, indeed, on their way to America, and the three of us would be some of the select few invited to the ranch.

Time-out: Let me take a moment to share how I got here. I'm the most recently saved out of our *Faith and Friction* crew. I was deeply immersed in the occult and New Age, searching for truth but unknowingly and dangerously entangled in darkness.

The spiritual realm has always been real to me. Long before I ever held a crystal or opened a Bible, I could feel things most people didn't, see shadows in the middle of the night, and hear whispers that made me think I was genuinely going crazy. I didn't have words for any of it until the New Age gave me language: empath, intuitive, awakening, higher power. I ate it up because it gave structure to the spiritual weirdness I had always felt.

Soon I was into chakras, energy alignment, mirror affirmations, manifestation, and astral projection. It felt mystical and empowering. But the more I pressed in, the more chaos followed. I couldn't sleep. I felt watched. I was tormented. And what promised peace brought deeper darkness.

That's the deception: It looks like healing and speaks of light, love, and wholeness, but behind the curtain is a seductive, ancient evil. I didn't see it. I was blinded. Until Jesus rescued me and my eyes were opened.

The veil in my spirit was lifted, and I encountered the Holy Spirit. My Abba Father called me home and I ran into His arms at the age of thirty-one. I remember asking a friend if she knew of a good local church. On the surface, it seemed like a casual question, but in reality, the Holy Spirit used her to speak to me.

She invited me to hers, and that's how I walked into the doors of my first church. The Holy Spirit seemed to meet me instantly. I encountered something I never had before, and I gave my life to Christ that day and was baptized shortly after. I didn't even know the Gospels yet, and I definitely couldn't name the disciples, but I knew spiritual warfare was real. Even without Christian language, I could feel that something bigger was happening. The war was here, and a greater war was coming.

I praise God that I've been drafted to the only undefeated franchise in all of history: Team Jesus. And honestly, with everything I've walked through—New Age deception, wild spiritual warfare, and some straight-up end times dreams—this whole red heifer journey and writing this book doesn't feel all that crazy. If anything, it feels exactly like where God has been leading me. Wild, yet makes perfect sense. And just a few years later, I was on a ranch in search of red heifers that are prophetic in nature. I wasn't sure where this ride would take me, but I was all in.

So here's my perspective of that day. It was December 20, 2021, a bright and early Monday morning, and Jason, Chichi, and I hopped in an SUV and took the hour-and-a-half road trip from Fort Worth to Rockwall, Texas. I sat in the back seat, documenting everything as it unfolded. I was asking questions and recording Jason as he explained the significance of the red heifers.

It was so easy for me to ask the most basic questions since I had no clue what was happening. *Who are these rabbis? Why Texas? What does this mean for us Christians? What does this mean for Jewish people? Are we connected to them? Where is this in Scripture? An animal is going to be sacrificed? What? Is this demonic? Should we be supporting this? Why?* All of the questions some of you may be asking probably happened in that car ride.

It was cool to watch Jason in his lane, spitting out wisdom and revelation the entire road trip. And it was a massive privilege to film this alongside my husband. I wasn't even sure what the end goal of our filming would be. A documentary? A podcast? A few clips?

As we neared our destination, a hush fell over us. The weight of what was happening really hit us. We drove down this long dirt road on the ranch, and we saw people gathering around the red heifers. We got out of the car and walked toward the group, taking it all in: the sharp bite of cold air, the smell of manure (as a Pennsylvania girl who grew up around farms, this smell was comfortably familiar), the mooing of the cows, and the tangible anticipation. Did I mention it was cold? Like, *really* cold. Uncomfortably cold. But that honestly didn't matter.

Then, shortly after we arrived, a few SUVs pulled in and out stepped the rabbis from Jerusalem. Mic check. Is this even real?

As time went by and introductions were made, there was a level of joy in the air that simply can't be described. Jews and Christians were standing side by side, getting ready to search every hair of the group of newly born red heifers.

Cameras and cell phones were recording every moment. Rabbis were explaining what they were looking for and the significance of the moment. They entered the bullpen and, alongside the ranch hand, they brought in one red heifer at a time. Jason stood in the middle of it all, boots muddied, his phone held high, FaceTiming rabbis back in Jerusalem.

I was on the outskirts of the pen with Chichi, cameras rolling. My fingers and toes were numb, but regardless of the cold, we moved in sync—one tracking the wide shot, the other capturing tight angles of the heifers' examinations. Every few moments, we turned to each other and exchanged an "are we really here right now?" look.

The weight of what we were documenting was not lost on us. This wasn't just another video shoot; it was potentially history in the making. I had a moment where I felt the Holy Spirit fall on me and tears welled up in my eyes in awe and reverence. The girl who didn't know Jesus four years prior was potentially standing in what felt like a page in the Bible.

The ranch hand moved with the quiet confidence of someone who had done this a thousand times, wrestling one red heifer to the ground at a time. The rabbis stepped in close, their eyes scanning every inch with precise care. The ranch hand kept the heifers steady as the rabbis combed through their coats, parting the thick red fur while inspecting for marks, scars, and discoloration. If a single white or black hair was found, the red heifer was deemed "unqualified" and was sent to the "no" pen. If the cow was deemed "pure," it was sent to the "yes" pen.

After a few hours of examination, seven red heifers were qualified as pure (only five remained qualified when they were sent to Israel). They weren't allowed to be tagged, since any mark that wasn't kosher would disqualify them. Someone on the ranch brought in orange chalk and wrote Hebrew letters or numbers on their foreheads, identifying them. It made the moment that much more surreal. Each symbol marked them. The thought came to my mind: *Is it possible that one of these red heifers, born at Triple Creek Ranch in Rockwall, Texas, could be the cow that gets sacrificed on Temple Mount? Is it possible that we are standing in biblical prophecy? Recording it with our own cameras and cell phones?*

While I don't walk in fear regarding the end times (though

sometimes I have my human moments), it does give me a deeper sense of urgency. I need to be sure that I know God's voice. I want to point people to Jesus when the chaos happens. I want people to trust God and what He's doing and not focus on what the Enemy is doing. No matter what happens, whether one of these cows gets sacrificed or not, Jesus sits on the throne. His name will be glorified. And I'm just in awe that I get to say I'm Abba's daughter—called and chosen for such a time as this.

Chichi Onyekanne

The idea of learning about eschatology, or end times, had been an odd obsession of mine for over a decade or so. Well, *obsession* may be too strong a word, but I would definitely be embarrassed if I was able to tally the total hours I've spent "rabbit-holing" YouTube videos about all this. There are so many different thoughts and perspectives when it comes to this topic, and it's easy to get lost in it all. But here I was, sitting in this SUV on my way to go film some red cows and rabbis. How does someone take that in?

I remember a friend texted me that day asking what I was up to because they wanted to hang out, and I had to think about how to respond. Do I hit them with the nonchalant, "Nothing, bro, just about to go film rabbis looking at red cows to take back to Israel to potentially sacrifice and likely impact the entire world as we know it, causing global conflict and potentially leading to the second coming of Jesus Christ?" No. I obviously kept it cool. But this subject was something of immense interest to me, and all of a sudden, I was inserted in the middle of what might turn out to be a pivotal part in it all.

As we pulled up to this ranch, I couldn't help but think of

how the last thirteen years had led to this moment. I remembered meeting Jason at my high school. He was a youth pastor then and was at the school pouring into and serving students. He approached me with what I assumed were Buckle pants and an Affliction button-up shirt. If you know, you know. He invited me to a youth event his church was having. Fast-forward a bit: I went to said event, got saved, and for the next few years Jason was my youth pastor and eventually my lead pastor.

But that's not the wild part to me (yes, there's something wilder than Buckle jeans). I remember Jason doing an end times / end-of-the-world series just months after I met him. For youth! Asking if our generation could be the one chosen to help set the stage for the return of Christ and how that would impact the way we lived. It was a frequent topic for our group. Not in the weird doomsday, turn-or-burn way but in the "what if you were chosen for such a time as this" way. And at this moment over a decade later, we were on a ranch with rabbis from Israel who, from the other side of the world, had been having the same conversations. It was an honor to have a front-row seat to a process that could ultimately have prophetic implications. So needless to say, this wasn't just another day for me!

Now, a look at that day from my perspective. There was a small group of people there. Maybe fifteen to twenty or so. My wife, Tracy, and I were tasked with documentation. I couldn't help but think that this was going to be a major thing with tons of people and news outlets present. But there was only one other camera crew. For them it was likely just their assignment for the day. For us? This was the start of a potentially history-shifting season. The search was officially on.

We watched and filmed as calf after calf was brought in to

be thoroughly examined by these rabbis. Every few moments the rabbis would address all the onlookers, explaining what was taking place and what they were looking for. It was amazing to see the excitement on their faces when they would approve one of the calves. I can't imagine what must have been going through their minds. Generations of anticipation had led to this moment. I would glance over to the "yes" pen from time to time and ask myself, *Could this actually be what we've talked about for years?* Tracy and I often stepped aside for side conversations to take it all in. It didn't sink in until much later. Would the red heifer come from this bunch? Would it come from a later bunch? Would it come from this ranch? One thing was for sure: We had a seat at the table and were in the thick of it.

When it was all said and done, there were seven red cows that had qualified. The excitement at this point on the ranch was evident. People were excited for different reasons. A collision of stories. There was even a moment I glanced over and one of the rabbis was frantically speaking to a group back in Israel on a video call. It wasn't in English, so I wasn't sure what the words meant, but the emotions were evident. I wasn't the only one who noticed this. Somone else looked over and asked a rabbi close by, "What's he saying to them?" Naturally I leaned in because inquiring minds wanted to know. One of the main rabbis there turned to look at the crowd and said, "He said, 'I think we found the red heifer.'" The group erupted in applause. I looked around and realized that the people were clapping for different reasons: One group was awaiting a messiah, and the other group was awaiting the return of a Messiah. But both events were affected by a red cow that could potentially be in the pen I was standing in. Yeah, I was a long way from the curious teen in a youth group end time series.

The process to find and sacrifice a perfect red heifer had officially begun. I didn't know then what this would mean for people around the world. But if this was what we thought—prophetic events potentially unfolding in real time—it would eventually reach the multitudes. Here was a ranch full of Jewish and Christian believers. Two storylines running parallel to each other with prophetic overlapping. I remember taking a group photo and thinking about the conversations that would be had in both groups of people. Despite the differences, this process was now in motion, and we had front-row seats.

Annaly Mawire

I've spent years under the teaching of my father-in-law, Dr. Robert Mawire, and I relished any opportunity to sit and converse about end-time prophecy, a topic that had fascinated me since I was young. Even as a child, I would have dreams about the end times—vivid, sometimes unsettling visions that stirred awe, curiosity, and a sense of urgency in my heart. There was something about God's unfolding plan for the world that captivated me even before I fully understood it. Even now, as I settled into a chair in Robert's living room, I could feel that familiar pull, the magnetic draw of deep theological discussion.

Marrying into Robert's family only deepened that fascination. Hearing his epic testimonies over the years, and meeting the very people who corroborated the events and prophetic insights he shared, made me realize that my path into this family was no accident. Each conversation, each account, confirmed that God had a purpose in aligning our paths. When I had the chance to visit Israel with them, the experience opened an entirely new perspective. I began digging deeper into Israel's history, the significance of biblical prophecy, and the intricate details surrounding the last days. It wasn't just academic; it felt alive, urgent, and intensely personal.

I remember that moment in his living room vividly. Robert leaned forward, eyes gleaming, and said, "I'm heading to Rockwall later today. A group of rabbis are coming to see some red heifers." Curiosity flickered within me, but in true Robert fashion, his unfazed delivery—after all, he deals with events of monumental significance on a regular basis—made the invitation feel almost casual. Add to that the fact that it was the middle of winter, the biting cold nudged me toward a polite decline. At the time, I didn't yet understand the full weight of the red heifers, their ceremonial importance, their prophetic significance, and I wasn't ready to grasp it fully. Looking back now, that invitation feels almost symbolic. Even in my absence, God had already begun weaving a tapestry I couldn't yet see.

Growing up as a pastor's kid in the West, the Jewish people and their role in biblical prophecy had never been central to my faith. They were mentioned, yes, but their significance, and their connection to the end times, had never been emphasized. As far as I understood, God's promises and focus had shifted entirely to the believers in Christ. Only later, through experience and study, did I realize how much I had overlooked. The very people I had once considered peripheral were, in fact, central to God's plan of redemption.

As my understanding deepened, I felt a growing desire to share what I was learning. I began speaking about these revelations on social media—small posts at first, little nuggets of insight— and the response surprised me. People were hungry for clarity, for truth, for a way to navigate the mysteries of the last days. It wasn't long before I launched a podcast, partnering with a cohost who shared my passion and curiosity. Remarkably, my first cohost had also been at the red heifer discovery, completely independent of the future *Faith and Friction* crew, who I'd meet later down the line. Ironically, the first episode of both podcasts focused on the red heifers.

The podcast began growing quickly, attracting listeners eager for insight and truth. Then life intervened: God led my cohost to move, and we had to pause the show. I took a break, but the pull to continue speaking on these topics never left me. A few months later, my family and I began visiting Jason's church, where I met Tracy, Chichi, and Jason. Jason, a lifelong friend of my husband and a fellow student of Dr. Robert Mawire, shared the same passion for prophecy and matched the energy and curiosity I had been missing.

Feeling prompted to continue this mission, I pulled Tracy aside and asked if she would join me in starting a new podcast. That's when the pieces of God's plan revealed themselves in an incredible way. Tracy shared that Chichi and Jason were also feeling led to launch a podcast and that all three of them had experienced the very same red heifer event at the ranch that had connected my first cohost and me months earlier. The realization was staggering. God had been orchestrating our paths behind the scenes, linking us through this extraordinary moment long before we ever met. It was a surreal confirmation that this new podcast was exactly what we were meant to do.

Together, we formed the *Faith and Friction* podcast team, combining our insights, our shared experiences with the red heifers, and our mutual passion for prophecy, Israel, and the mysteries of the last days. The coincidences and divine timing felt undeniable, reinforcing the sense that every step of this journey was part of a greater plan. Each of our stories and separate experiences had been part of a larger design leading to this. And fittingly, the very first episode of *Faith and Friction* explored that connection, the red heifers—cementing not just the topic but the bond that would define our work together. Holy cow, literally!

And Now, Back to Your Regularly Scheduled Programming

Back to the goal of this book and back to one voice! An unlikely team. An ancient search. And prophecy in motion. Different roads led us to this very moment. What started as a hunger for a greater understanding of biblical prophecy, prayers, YouTube rabbit holes, and so much more created this very book. We started our podcast, *Faith and Friction*, in hopes of inviting people into deeper conversation and understanding of biblical prophecy and how it may be related to some of the headlines that were surfacing around the world—to help the church navigate these topics and be confident of their understanding when future headlines emerge. We know that our salvation was final and cemented in the death and resurrection of Jesus as the last sacrifice. Because of that, we can lean into these conversations and take this journey through Scripture and history. So stick with us! It gets interesting.

There may have been a dozen different reasons you've decided to pick up this book. Maybe you read an intriguing headline, maybe you're a podcast listener and were already sold, maybe you think all of this is dumb and want to confirm how dumb it all is, or maybe you just liked the cover and wanted to see what it was about. However you got here, welcome! Welcome to a space where biblical prophecy meets an Indiana Jones-esque adventure and investigation. We'll answer questions you're sure to have (trust us, a lot of you will have even more questions) and journey through lots of scriptures and historic texts to see where it all points. We ask that you take this journey with us and pray about what conclusions the Lord may have you draw. Read straight through, skip around, or go to the Glossary and the FAQs in the back—the choice is yours. But know that if in fact the pages of this book truly reflect things of prophetic proportion, what a journey it'll be!

Now let's go ahead and address some questions you probably have already: If Jesus Christ was the final sacrifice for our sins once and for all, then why in the world are we talking about sacrificing cows? If the Holy Spirit dwells in us upon receiving salvation, why are we mentioning another temple? These are very valid questions.

We believe and hold steadfast to the fact and truth that Jesus Christ died for our sins as the last and *final* sacrifice for the atonement of sin forever. Did you get that? Jesus was the last sacrifice necessary for our sins. Lock that in as you journey through the rest of the book. The things we are going to talk about and cover are not in relation to salvation. We believe that was completed in Jesus and His finished work at the cross and that the only way to the Father is through Him. This book is about *prophecy* we believe the Scriptures have laid out for us. This book wasn't written to try to predict the exact moment Jesus is going to return or offer an exact timeline for prophetic apocalyptic events. This book was written to invite you on a journey through Scripture and history. To ask questions. To challenge claims. Yes, ours included. We want to instigate a more robust view of Scripture as it pertains to things you likely won't hear about in a Sunday morning message.

We don't know about you guys, but there seems to be an echo that has rung out in the church about the times we're in. More and more people are asking if we are in the "last days." And sure, people have been talking about these days since Jesus ascended back into heaven, but what does the Bible actually say about those "days"? Now, it is very clear no one knows the day and hour, but we believe it's also clear that we ought to know the season. We promise we'll dive into those scriptures a little more later, but for now let's get back to these red cows.

If you would have told us five years ago that we'd be writing a book on red cows, end times, and biblical prophecy, we all probably would have shared a confused look and laughed. Ask any Western Christian their list of "top five most important events concerning end-time prophecy" and you'll probably get the usual responses like the Antichrist, the false prophet, the mark of the beast, Jesus on a white horse, maybe even a dragon . . . But a cow? Out of all the wild and mind-blowing topics in biblical prophecy, a cow wouldn't have made our list either. But the events that transpired were nothing short of divine—so divinely orchestrated, in fact, that the only explanation we were left with was, "God must be doing something!" Isn't it like God to use the most seemingly insignificant things of this world to signify the grandness of His biblical fulfillments and prophecies, so much so that if you weren't paying attention, you'd miss it? If you're asking, Why would a red cow used for Jewish ceremonial purposes be such a prophetic trigger? You are not alone! Let's jump into the history of all this.

CHAPTER 2

COULD A COW REALLY SHAKE NATIONS?

The Prophetic Puzzle Piece Few Are Talking About

"The Unlikely Role Red Cows Play in War Between Israel and Hamas."[1] That's the title of a CBS News video released about five months after Hamas attacked Israel on October 7, 2023. Why would cows have a role in a war? Sounds crazy, right? Here's an excerpt from that article to provide you with a deeper level of understanding of the magnitude of what took place.

> When Hamas spokesman Abu Ubaida began a speech marking the 100th day of the war in Gaza, one confounding yet eye-opening proclamation escaped the headlines. Listing the motives for the Palestinian militant group's Oct. 7 massacre in Israel, he accused Jews of "bringing red cows" to the Holy Land.
>
> The cows he was talking about are red heifers, which now graze at a secure, undisclosed location in the Israeli-occupied

> West Bank. Some Jews and Christians believe they're key to rebuilding the Jewish temple that once stood in Jerusalem, and to beckoning the Messiah.
>
> To understand, you have to look back almost 2,000 years in the tumultuous history of the Middle East, when the ancient Romans destroyed the last temple in Jerusalem.
>
> To rebuild it, fervent believers point to the Bible's Book of Numbers, which commands the Israelites to offer "a red heifer without defect or blemish and that has never been under a yoke." Only with that offering, they insist, can the temple rise again.[2]

If your introduction to red heifers in relation to end times or Christianity has only happened in recent years, or maybe just now, don't worry, you're not alone. While topics like the Third Temple, the Antichrist, the mark of the beast, wars, white horses, the prophetic timeline found in Daniel, and even dragons may be more familiar to you (and rest assured, we'll get into some of these things later in this book), the idea of cows playing a pivotal role might seem unexpected. Yet, in order for any of those more commonly discussed events to unfold, the first essential step is the identification and sacrifice of a perfect, unblemished, and never-yoked red heifer. Like we said before—not for salvation but for fulfillment of prophecy.

An entire prophetic road map hinges on the presence of a single, specific animal. It's a requirement of such monumental significance that the process has already sparked controversy and global tensions.

We pray that through this book you would have confidence navigating discussions surrounding the potential headlines of tomorrow, and the headlines of recent years as well. We are going to dig in to a lot of things that surround these conversations. What does Scripture say about it all? What is the media saying about it? Where does the church go from here? We're getting into all of it!

Many people have been under the impression that the Christian church has replaced the Jewish people altogether under the new covenant. But what if their significance to end-time prophecy is greater than we imagined?

Many people have been under the impression that the Christian church has replaced the Jewish people altogether under the new covenant. But what if their significance to end-time prophecy is greater than we imagined?

Where Prophecy Meets the Pages: The Red Heifer in the Bible

So where in the Bible is all this red heifer stuff actually located? That would probably be a great place to start, right? In Numbers 19, a unique and important purification ceremony is described, and part of that ceremony required a specific type of cow. God instructed Moses to sacrifice a perfect, unblemished red heifer and use its ashes to purify people who had become ritually unclean, especially those who had come in contact with a dead body.

Before we go further, go ahead and grab your Bible (or read the passage in full on pages 28 and 29) and let's read Numbers 19:1–19.

Numbers 19:1–19

Now the LORD spoke to Moses and Aaron, saying, "This *is* the ordinance of the law which the LORD has commanded, saying: 'Speak to the children of Israel, that they bring you a red heifer without blemish, in which there *is* no defect *and* on which a yoke has never come. You shall give it to Eleazar the priest, that he may take it outside the camp, and it shall be slaughtered before him; and Eleazar the priest shall take some of its blood with his finger, and sprinkle some of its blood seven times directly in front of the tabernacle of meeting. Then the heifer shall be burned in his sight: its hide, its flesh, its blood, and its offal shall be burned. And the priest shall take cedar wood and hyssop and scarlet and cast *them* into the midst of the fire burning the heifer. Then the priest shall wash his clothes, he shall bathe in water, and afterward he shall come into the camp; the priest shall be unclean until evening. And the one who burns it shall wash his clothes in water, bathe in water, and shall be unclean until evening. Then a man *who is* clean shall gather up the ashes of the heifer, and store *them* outside the camp in a clean place; and they shall be kept for the congregation of the children of Israel for the water of purification; it *is* for purifying from sin. And the one who gathers the ashes of the heifer shall wash his clothes, and be unclean until evening. It shall be a statute forever to the children of Israel and to the stranger who dwells among them.

'He who touches the dead body of anyone shall be unclean seven days. He shall purify himself with the water on the third day and on the seventh day; *then* he will be clean. But if he does not purify himself on the third day and on the seventh day, he will not be clean. Whoever touches the body of anyone who has died, and does not purify himself, defiles the tabernacle of the Lord. That person shall be cut off from Israel. He shall be unclean, because the water of purification was not sprinkled on him; his uncleanness *is* still on him.

'This *is* the law when a man dies in a tent: All who come into the tent and all who *are* in the tent shall be unclean seven days; and every open vessel, which has no cover fastened on it, *is* unclean. Whoever in the open field touches one who is slain by a sword or who has died, or a bone of a man, or a grave, shall be unclean seven days.

'And for an unclean *person* they shall take some of the ashes of the heifer burnt for purification from sin, and running water shall be put on them in a vessel. A clean person shall take hyssop and dip *it* in the water, sprinkle *it* on the tent, on all the vessels, on the persons who were there, or on the one who touched a bone, the slain, the dead, or a grave. The clean *person* shall sprinkle the unclean on the third day and on the seventh day; and on the seventh day he shall purify himself, wash his clothes, and bathe in water; and at evening he shall be clean.'"

Can we just take a quick moment and acknowledge how much Scripture that was? We know it's a lot. And it may not be the most exciting chapter you've read in the Bible, but as we journey into this book, you'll understand how the process described is crucial to understanding why this red heifer is necessary, so hang tight.

So why is this important? Well, for the ancient Israelites, staying clean in a spiritual and ritual sense was vital for participating in worship and other sacred activities. The red heifer, which had to be completely red and without any defects or blemishes, was sacrificed, and its ashes were then mixed with water. This special mixture was sprinkled on people who needed purification, helping them become "clean" again to be able to engage in the temple and its rituals. This ritual wasn't just about physical cleanliness; it had to do with restoring a person's spiritual purity.

The red heifer's significance stretches far beyond just a one-time ritual. In Jewish tradition, there's a belief that the next arrival of a perfect red heifer is a sign of the eventual rebuilding of the Third Temple in Jerusalem (again, we'll get to all the drama surrounding the Third Temple later). This is why the red heifer has continued to capture the interest of Jewish communities for centuries.

For Christians, the red heifer in Scripture could easily be seen as a type and shadow of Jesus. We know that He was spotless and without blemish and was sacrificed for our redemption. But could this red heifer represent something totally different for Jews today?

The Mishnah and the Red Heifers

Have you ever watched the sequel of a movie without seeing the first one? There can be gaps—holes—in your understanding of what's happening. Or what about prequels that come out years after the original movie series and piece the whole story together for you? Consider this history lesson on the red heifers a prequel of sorts, something that will hopefully piece things together. You may have been a follower of Christ for years, maybe even decades, and have never heard about this. Or maybe you're new to faith, and all of this may have just thrown the biggest curveball at you. Don't worry, we're almost at the end of our history lesson.

Over the years, there have been nine known red heifers that were sacrificed, each marking an important moment in history. Understanding the story of these nine sacrifices helps set the stage for the ongoing anticipation of the tenth red heifer, an event that many believe will play a significant role in fulfilling biblical prophecy. Although Numbers 19 is the sole chapter in the Bible that goes into depth regarding this ancient ritual, Jewish traditions, oral laws, and practices have been documented and preserved by various means. There are a couple of Jewish texts that are foundational and expound in more detail about the previous nine red heifers that have been found and sacrificed. One of those texts is the Mishnah.

The Mishnah is a foundational text in Jewish tradition, often regarded as the first major written compilation of the oral law that had been passed down through generations of Jewish teachers. While it is obviously not part of the Bible itself, the Mishnah serves as an essential guide to understanding how the Jewish people have interpreted and applied biblical teachings, especially in areas like law, ritual, and worship. The Mishnah might be unfamiliar to Christians, but it offers valuable context for understanding the cultural and religious practices that shaped the world of Jesus and the early church.

When it comes to the red heifer and its associated sacrifices, the Mishnah provides detailed explanations about the specific requirements for the animal, the purification rituals, and how these practices were performed in ancient times. While the Mishnah doesn't hold the same status as the Bible, it plays a crucial role in understanding how ancient Jews lived out their faith and adhered to the laws of purity, making it a resource for anyone studying biblical rituals, including those concerning the red heifer. By exploring the Mishnah, we gain deeper insight into the religious mindset and practices of the time. It enhances our understanding of prophetic scriptures and how they relate to Jewish expectations of temple restoration and, for Christians, the fulfillment of prophecy through Jesus Christ as well as His return. We're not saying you should go download the Mishnah on your Kindle and start a study, but we are saying that it can fill in gaps on how Christianity and Jewish beliefs overlap. Again, this isn't pertaining to salvation but rather biblical prophecy.

Let's jump into a brief history of the first nine red heifers for a little context. The info for the red heifers is not only found in the Mishnah but collected and documented in the Jewish Virtual Library. Here are some brief summaries that will help you understand how deep this red heifer stuff goes historically. This isn't new or random. This was a tradition and practice known and understood for generations.

The Mishnah Parah 3:5 states the first red heifer dates back to the time of Moses, after the Israelites' exodus from Egypt.[3] According to tradition, the red heifer of this period was sacrificed as part of the purification process following the construction of the tabernacle. The ashes from this heifer would have been used for the purification of the people, particularly for those who were ceremonially unclean due to contact with death. This event is significant because it marks the first recorded instance of the red heifer sacrifice and because it sets the precedent for the ritual that would be observed by the Israelites in the centuries to come. Imagine if the Israelites in DreamWorks's *The Prince of Egypt* had stuck around for the red heifer scene. One minute you're singing "When You Believe," the next you're watching Moses explain how to burn a cow and save the ashes. Holy barbecue anyone?

The second red heifer sacrifice is believed to have occurred during the time the First Temple was built in Jerusalem. This red heifer was prepared by the prophet Ezra. The historical significance of this red heifer lies in its role in preparing the people for the consecration of the First Temple, an event that holds great importance in Jewish history.

The third through ninth red heifer sacrifices all occurred during the time and era of the Second Temple up until it was destroyed in AD 70. According to the Mishnah, there are several priests who prepared those seven heifers during Second Temple times. Shimon the Just and Yochanan each prepared two. El'yhoeini ben Hakof, Chanamel HaMitzri, and Yishmael ben Pi'avi processed one heifer each (if you skipped over some of those names, we don't blame you at all).

Since the destruction of the Second Temple, the Jewish people have hoped and longed for the next spotless red heifer. A twelfth-century rabbi by the name of Moshe ben Maimon was considered by Jews to be one of the greatest Jewish scholars of all time. His writing still heavily influences Judaism today. He authored the Mishneh Torah, a fourteen-volume code of Jewish law, where he detailed the previous nine red heifer findings. And in it he made a bold statement. He wrote, "The tenth red heifer will be prepared by the King Messiah. May he be revealed speedily, Amen, may it be God's will."[4] The Jewish people believe that the tenth red heifer will be sacrificed in the era of the coming of their messiah. Some even say that their messiah will be the one to sacrifice it.

But why after all these years (thousands of years, to be clear) are they just now looking for this red heifer? Well, another brief history lesson is in order. Don't worry, this one will feel way more relevant to things that you may have seen or heard about. But basically, the Jewish people didn't own the land. Let's get into why.

Years after the destruction of the Second Temple, sometime around AD 135, the Roman emperor Hadrian essentially kicked the Jews out of Jerusalem. The Jewish people were under Roman rule and decided to revolt. One of the uprisings was known as the Bar Kokhba Revolt, named after a charismatic figure who was stirring the pot and encouraging other Jews to rise up. This uprising was working at first but ultimately resulted in several casualties and a big "L" for the Jews. As a result, Hadrian sold imprisoned Jews into slavery, forbade the teaching of the Torah, and renamed the province Syria Palestina. Over 1,500 years would go by before the Jews regained control of what they believed was their ancestral homeland.[5]

For over a thousand years the territory was under Muslim and Arab rule. Despite there being some remaining Jews, the majority of the land was Arab. With Jewish people longing to return to the land of their ancestors, the Zionist movement was birthed. Now this is a term you may have heard thrown around social media and the news. In the simplest terms, it was a movement created to bring Jews back to Israel. With the hatred of Jews across Europe and Russia, the push to return grew. More and more Jews immigrated to the land and were met by Arabs who considered it the land of their ancestors also. Long story short, after a bunch of conflict and multiple changes in power, the state of Israel was established in 1948.

So the reason they hadn't looked for a red heifer for all this time is, well, they couldn't. Not until they had the land again. According to Jewish law, the sacrifice and preparation of the red heifer's ashes must take place in the land of Israel, in connection with the temple. For centuries they had neither the land nor the temple, so the command couldn't be carried out. Since 1948, the Jewish people have searched for this red heifer on numerous occasions. Apparently, it's way harder to find a completely pure red heifer than you might think. But the search was on. And it led to a group of Jewish rabbis visiting a Red Angus ranch in Texas.

Now, hearing all of that may cause you to be intrigued, or maybe you've been rolling your eyes the whole time you've been reading. You may have even skipped to this part. We welcome it all. As the climate in the Middle East surrounding Israel, which has always been at the center of global prophetic and historic events, seems to always be a moment away from conflict or chaos, we believe the Word of God has gone before us. So as we dive into it, we pray it comes alive in a new way for you as well!

Coffee Break and Recap

Okay, that was a lot of information. Feel free to take a break, grab a coffee, and just exhale. Or maybe you're moved to go down an even deeper history rabbit hole based on what you just learned. To that we say, go for it! It's important to establish certain foundations. And as we take this investigative journey together, we don't just want you to take our word for it. We invite you to research, ask questions, and let the Holy Spirit lead you into understanding. You won't hurt our feelings, we promise! This isn't a new concept. This isn't something we just decided to pick up because we felt maybe a book needed to be written about this, so we thought we'd see what we could squeeze out. We were on a journey like you are now, and we hope this book can provide further insight.

Let's do a quick recap! The red heifer sacrifice is one of the most unique and sacred rituals in Jewish tradition, with specific requirements that must be met for the ritual to be valid. First and foremost, the heifer must be completely red with no more than two non-red hairs and free from any physical blemishes or defects. It can't have ever been used for work. The heifer was and will be sacrificed outside the temple precincts, in a designated sacred area, and then completely burned by a qualified priest. The priest performing the ritual must be ritually pure and typically a descendant of Aaron, ensuring the sacrifice follows the correct lineage and spiritual standards (all of these things have also been in the works! Crazy!).

After the red heifer is slaughtered and burned, its ashes are carefully collected and mixed with water, which becomes the purification mixture used to cleanse individuals who are ritually impure. The ashes are sprinkled on the unclean person, restoring their spiritual purity. Then they are allowed to participate in temple worship and reconnect with God. Remember that scripture passage you might've skipped earlier? Observant Jews still hold tightly to the command in Numbers 19. That passage makes it clear: The ashes of a red heifer are the key to purification from ritual impurity, especially for anyone who's come into contact with death, which after thousands of years, is essentially everyone. Without those ashes, they can't be considered ritually clean, which means they can't take part in temple worship when it's restored. So if the temple is going to be rebuilt, the purification process must come first, and that starts with a red heifer.

We believe this has so much more to do with believers in Christ than you may know or think. So strap in, we're just getting started. And for the record, just in case you missed it, we believe that Jesus was the final sacrifice for our sins and upon receiving salvation we are invited into eternal life. This book won't change your role as a Christian and believer. But hopefully it will increase your urgency to carry out the Great Commission and be used by God to build His kingdom!

CHAPTER 3

IS THE RED HEIFER THE FIRST DOMINO?

How One Ancient Ritual Sets Off a Chain of Prophetic Events

We've thrown a lot of history at you, but it's important to know that what's taking place isn't just some new idea that a random and likely unrelatable end times group came up with. This has been a significant event throughout history. Not only has it been something that we've been tracking for years, it's also crazy to think that we were actually there for the initiation of a process that will end up being a major event as it pertains to prophecy. And if there's even a slight chance that what people have said and believe to be true is happening in our lifetime, shouldn't we want to know what's going on?

Let's start with something simple, shall we? Dominoes. Have you ever watched one of those elaborate domino videos on YouTube—the ones where a single flick sets off an epic chain reaction, eventually knocking over something potentially massive, like a life-sized block at the end of the chain? You can't help but watch the entire thing every time it comes across your screen. There's so much anticipation as the first domino is about to fall because you know what's going to happen next. Well, where we are in history, the red heifer might just be that first domino. Except this domino is ancient, sacred, and more consequential than your average game night. This domino will set off a chain of events that is sure to impact people around the world.

The sacrifice of the red heifer isn't merely ceremonial; it's the foundational act, the prologue to everything that follows. It's the season opener—episode one, chapter one. It is, in fact, the first domino. Without this spotless red cow, the dominoes of prophetic events leading into what many call the "Messianic Age" simply cannot fall into place. For this reason, the red heifer's role is not just symbolic but critical, standing as the inaugural indicator that sets the stage for this long-awaited new era.

This time period represents an era that the Jewish people have anticipated for thousands of years. We had the opportunity to engage in conversations with some individuals who were born and raised within the Jewish faith, exploring their thoughts and experiences in the anticipation of this historic occurrence. Their sentiments, while personal and nuanced, seemed to share a remarkable similarity. The selection of the tenth red heifer is not just an event to them; it is a culmination of centuries of dreams, prayers, and deep spiritual longing. For many, this moment serves as a bridge between their enduring hope for the arrival of the Messiah and the broader eschatological beliefs shared by others.

As believers in Jesus Christ, this crossroad challenges us

to consider how the fulfillment of their expectations intertwines with our anticipation of the second coming of Christ. As Christians, we believe Jesus was in fact the Messiah and that He will return again. Orthodox Jews don't believe Jesus was the Messiah and are still awaiting the arrival of their messiah; therefore, a temple is still needed for the atonement of sins for the people.

So here's where these stories overlap: Based on Scripture, there seem to be events that will precede the second coming of Christ (we'll deep dive into this later). And when those events happen, we can be confident in the times that we're in. But get this: Our signs for the second coming of Jesus are some of their signs for the first coming of their messiah. But according to the Bible (2 Thessalonians 2:3–4), this won't be a messiah after all.

The significance of this moment can't be overstated, as it holds profound meaning for both Jewish and Christian communities. With the red heifer seen as the initial domino in the unfolding of the Messianic Age, we found ourselves presented with a profound question: Could this be the moment when history allows the domino to tip, setting into motion events that have been foretold for generations for both Jews and Christians alike?

Throughout history, numerous individuals and groups have sought to pinpoint the timing of the second coming or to accurately predict the rapture, often employing a variety of methods and interpretations. Some may recall the infamous book *88 Reasons Why the Rapture Will Be in 1988* by Edgar C. Whisenant.[1] Whisenant, using a mix of numerology and personal study, confidently asserted his prediction, capturing the attention of millions worldwide. The book's popularity created a sense of urgency, with many on edge throughout that year. Can you imagine the kind of buzz this would have received if social media was in play? And obviously, spoiler alert, it didn't happen. However, predictions like these did not stop with 1988.

Year after year, new end times and doomsday forecasts have emerged, each tied to significant dates or cultural moments. The turn of the millennium—Y2K—had people hoarding bottled water and stockpiling canned goods. Then again in 2012, the Mayan calendar was set to end, and it seemed like all of a sudden their calendar became a global compass of time and existence. In the fall of 2025 some people turned one man's September rapture prediction into a global TikTok phenomenon.[2] So many political and societal events, such as elections, wars, blood moons, eclipses, or any other major global shift, have been used to spike fear or predict prophecy. Can you imagine being born around 1970, having your adulthood consistently marked by a rotating door of apocalyptic panics? "It's all ending! My bad, false alarm. Oh wait! It's all ending!" Talk about exhausting. These moments, though they have come and gone, serve as a reminder of humanity's enduring desire to understand and prepare for what lies ahead. You've heard the predictions before, and no doubt, you'll hear them again.

So, you might ask, why bother with yet another book talking about the end times? How is this book going to end up any different from the numerous books and articles written over the past century? Great question. Here's our promise: We won't aim to predict the exact day and hour Jesus is going to return; that would be contrary to Scripture. Instead, our goal is to *reverse engineer* the events leading up to Christ's return, based on Scripture, helping believers recognize the "dominoes" that must fall before that pivotal moment arrives—some of which you may not have been aware of.

Take Matthew 24, for example. You know the verse: "No one knows the day or hour" (v. 36 NLT). So many end-time conversations have been shut down with this line. It's served as a trump card for so long. If you've never used this line, you've surely heard it before. But being the intrepid investigators we are, we decided to dig into the original Greek. After long and extensive study, reflection, prayer, and fasting, we got it. And guess what it means? Are you ready for this? It simply means "day or hour." It means no one knows if Jesus is returning next Tuesday at 2:00 p.m. No one is putting a gold star on any future day on a calendar. But here's the catch: Though we can't know the exact moment, Scripture tells us that we should recognize the season.

Paul, in 1 Thessalonians 5:4, confirms this beautifully, urging believers to stay alert and recognize signs. Essentially, he was saying, "Don't be caught binge-watching Netflix when the big dominoes start falling."

The famous revivalist and theologian Jonathan Edwards once said: "Resolved, never to do anything, which I should be afraid to do, if I expected it would not be above an hour before I should hear the last trump."[3]

In other words, Edwards wanted to make sure that everything he was doing would be pleasing to the Lord. He aimed to live as if he knew the end was near, to be caught doing what he believed the Lord would want him doing. This is how Paul was urging us to live when these days arrive. But we'll unpack some of that later when we talk about the rapture and tribulation. (Oh yeah, we're definitely going there.)

First Things First

Let's zoom in on a particular domino, shall we? In 2 Thessalonians 2:3–4, Paul drops a pretty hefty clue: The Antichrist will set himself up in God's temple. The passage reads, "Don't let anyone deceive you in any way, for that day will not come until the rebellion occurs and the man of lawlessness is revealed, the man doomed to destruction. He will oppose and will exalt himself over everything that is called God or is worshiped, so that he sets himself up in God's temple, proclaiming himself to be God" (NIV).

Now that sounds like a domino. Paul says that until this event in 2 Thessalonians 2 happens, Jesus isn't going to return. If the Antichrist is taking selfies in the temple, posting them on Instagram with hashtags like #NewGodWhoDis, then logically, there must be a literal temple built beforehand. And in order for such a temple to come into existence and be properly consecrated, that temple needs purification from water and ashes: Enter stage left, our red heifer. And, in order to have those ashes, you guessed it, there has to be a sacrifice.

At each step in this prophetic chain, we see a much larger narrative unfolding. Indeed, some groups have gone to astonishing lengths to either accelerate or prevent these events from taking place. What might initially seem like a minor detail—the fate of a single red cow—quickly becomes a central element in a global conversation about eschatology. And as we continue to reverse engineer the signs leading up to Jesus' return, the ripples caused by this one domino only grow wider and more significant.

Now here's where things get fascinatingly complicated. According to recent headlines, such as that eyebrow-raising CBS article we discussed earlier, bringing red cows into Israel allegedly triggered one of the most severe conflicts in half a century. At first glance, it may seem implausible that a few cows could spur such a massive conflict. However, some people groups understand the ripple effect that will transpire once this takes place.

For Orthodox Jews, these heifers are the key to constructing the Third Temple. This cow will be a sign of temple preparation advancing. For many Muslims, however, these cows represent a threat to sacred sites: the Dome of the Rock and Al-Aqsa Mosque, which are currently occupying the Temple Mount. This is where the tension lies. The spot where the Jewish temple once stood and where many believe it must be rebuilt is the same area where those sacred Muslim sites currently are. And these aren't just historically important places Muslims would visit like a museum. These are two of the holiest sites in Islam.

So when talks of rebuilding a temple arise, people have very different responses. People are on edge. The red heifers being raised in Israel right now are a symbol that temple plans are getting real. And that causes friction. If you're a Muslim, the idea that your sacred sites could be replaced or disrupted feels like a direct attack on your faith. If you're a Jew preparing for the messiah, this feels like prophecy in motion. So yeah, it's definitely not just about cows. It's about prophecy, land, power, and even identity. This topic is spiritual firewood, just waiting for a spark. And this cow might just be the spark that sets everything off.

If the Jewish community continues to pursue construction of the Third Temple on land currently occupied by sacred Muslim sites, the October 2023 attack could indeed be just the tip of the iceberg of what's to come. Mustafa Abu Sway, a prayer leader at Al-Aqsa, aptly described this tension as "a Pandora's box that nobody can close," acknowledging the profound religious implications at play.[4] This area on Temple Mount is tightly guarded, restricting access so that only Muslims are permitted inside. When viewed in this light, one can easily envision how the arrival of a handful of red cows could ignite widespread apprehension and spark the kind of international tensions we're now witnessing and will likely continue to witness.

Some people believe this may only be the beginning. As believers, we already know how the story ends. We even recognize some of the events that pave the way to its conclusion, but understanding how these timelines begin can help us make sense of tomorrow's headlines.

For Jews, the ultimate hope has always been the arrival of who they believe will be their messiah, and they fully anticipate opposition and even further attacks. Meanwhile, Christians have long been taught that the end times are closer than ever. These two distinct narratives, with their own perspectives and outcomes, converge with yet another people group's story, creating a complex tapestry of faith, prophecy, and expectation. None of this is new: The conflict in the Middle East has spanned thousands of years, woven through layers of religious devotion, cultural identity, and historical legacy that continue to influence the events of our present day.

So many questions can arise from this information—questions you've likely been pondering ever since you picked up this book, or perhaps well before you began this journey with us. We want to emphasize that our purpose here is not to spark fear or anxiety but rather to educate the body of Christ on how these events align with the Word of God. Prophecy doesn't exist to

> **Prophecy doesn't exist to scare us; it exists to prepare us.**

scare us; it exists to prepare us. The beautiful truth is that we already know how the story ends: Ultimate victory is assured in Christ. We're journeying *from* victory, not *for* it. Even if the Lord tarries, our role as believers remains the same. And even more importantly, the road map of events before His return also remains the same.

Even as we were writing this book, something major happened in July of 2025. A practice red heifer sacrifice took place in Israel. And the internet lost it. Articles, organizations, and even several YouTubers jumped in to debate its meaning (seriously, if you Google it, brace yourself).[5] Some said it was just a practice run, while others wondered if this might've actually been the real thing.

We interviewed Byron Stinson, who was there, on our podcast to discuss the details.[6] This conversation did not disappoint. The way that it went down is sure to get you thinking. The details surrounding this practice sacrifice were fascinating. But here's what matters. The process isn't "someday" anymore—it's now. Prophecy is no longer distant. It's unfolding in real time.

So even if Jesus doesn't return for another one hundred years, and red heifers for the next decade get disqualified, the red heifer selection and sacrifice will continue to be the first domino that officially kicks everything off. Everything we'll talk about in this book will always hinge on a red heifer coming first. So it's important to know and be able to identify, through Scripture, what these dominoes will be.

Gaining a deeper understanding of end-time topics does not change our mission; rather, it refines our perspective. We are still commissioned, just as Matthew 28 instructs us, to make disciples of all nations. If anything, it should birth a new level of urgency for the Great Commission. Even so, we should remain mindful of the global events unfolding around us, whether they involve red heifers, the construction of the Third Temple, the Antichrist, or other eschatological developments. Our hope is that by learning about these topics, you will become more confident in your grasp of both Scripture and history, empowering you to face the potential times ahead with faith and wisdom.

Are you still tracking with us? Is your head spinning yet? We realize that new questions may continue to surface for you as you read on, and we welcome them wholeheartedly. Our desire is to help guide you through the details and bring as much clarity as possible to these complex subjects.

For over a decade, we've been discussing these matters and their significance, gathering insights to share with fellow believers who long to understand God's unfolding plan. At the end of this book, you'll find a QR code linking you to an online hub of resources on the red heifer and all the topics covered in this book. Scan it anytime to explore deeper studies, ask your questions, and connect with a community of believers continuing the conversation. In a world where headlines change daily, staying connected and informed helps us stand firm in faith, knowing that our God is at work even in the most challenging circumstances.

CHAPTER 4

JUDAISM 101: A CRASH COURSE YOU DIDN'T KNOW YOU NEEDED

Understanding Jewish Identity and God's Covenant

One of the most common questions on our platform is, "Why are you guys partnering with and trying to help nonbelievers? Jewish people don't believe and accept Jesus as the Messiah, so why are y'all trying to partner with them to bring a cow and build a temple?" Or another one we often get: "Why are y'all trying to bring the Antichrist? This is so demonic!" Crazy, right? Or maybe you have had the same thoughts as you went through these pages.

Are the Jewish people today the same people Scripture talks about? Is this current Israel actually the Israel God still has a promise for? Is a nation's government always in line with what God is saying? Is this some type of political agenda to pledge undying allegiance to a nation and its government and political structures and leaders?

Let's take a step back for a second. There is definitely a lot to unpack here. But the Gentiles and believers of today haven't simply replaced the Jewish people in God's plan like many may think. We invite you to journey through Scripture with us a bit. What does the Bible actually say about the Jewish people, especially when it comes to end-time fulfillment? If we're being honest, all of it can get pretty confusing. No worries, we get it. But in order to understand and grasp what the Bible says about prophecy, we have to know about the Jews. It's foundational to the road map of the end times.

Have you found yourself asking, "Wait, if Jesus and His disciples were Jewish, why do so many Jewish people today not believe in Jesus? When did that split happen? Would the real Jewish people please stand up?!" These are really good questions—the kind that have puzzled people for years. And here's the thing: Getting clarity on some of these questions isn't just interesting history. It's crucial for understanding Bible prophecy. So grab your coffee (or whatever you're drinking), and let's dive into this together. We're going to trace the story of the Jewish people from the very beginning and figure out exactly who they are and why it matters so much for understanding where we're headed.

It All Started with Abraham

To understand Jewish identity, we need to go all the way back to a man named Abraham (his name was Abram until Genesis 17, when God changed his name). You may be familiar with him—this is the Father Abraham who had many sons. And many sons had Father Abraham! (Shout-out to all the Sunday school kids who sang that song! Can we bring it back?) Around four thousand years ago, God called Abraham to leave everything he knew and go to a place that He would show him. Abraham had to leave his city, his people, his father's home, everything. And God didn't tell him where he was going. It's crazy to think about the magnitude of this ask. It reminds us of Jesus calling the disciples: "Follow Me. Don't worry about where we're going. Let's go." But this wasn't just about moving to a new city. God made an incredible promise to Abraham that would shape history.

God told Abraham, "I will make you into a great nation, and I will bless you; I will make your name great, and you will be a blessing. I will bless those who bless you, and whoever curses you I will curse; and all peoples on earth will be blessed through you" (Genesis 12:2–3 NIV). This was the beginning of what is called the Abrahamic covenant, God's special relationship with Abraham and his descendants.

But here's something fascinating that most people might miss: This covenant was actually ratified in a very unusual way. In Genesis 15:8–21, Abraham asks God what proof he'll have that he will inherit the land. God responds by telling Abraham to bring him specific animals for sacrifice and then putting him into a deep sleep. In verse 17 Scripture says there was a flaming torch that passed through the sacrifices. We can take a moment to acknowledge that's actually pretty wild—the presence of God waltzing through these animal sacrifices. But as we dug deeper, we uncovered an interesting fact that changed the story for us.

In ancient times, when two parties made a covenant, both of the parties would walk between the sacrificed animals together, essentially saying, "May what happened to these animals happen to me if I break this covenant." This was commonly known as a "cutting covenant."[1] In this case, God seems to make what looks like a one-sided covenant. Abraham, as customs understood, didn't walk through the sacrifices. He didn't commit to "holding up his end of the bargain." God was the One who made the promise and was the One who fulfilled the "act" of committing to uphold that covenant promise.

Have you ever signed a contract while you were unconscious? Yeah, neither have we. But that's exactly what happened with Abraham. God put him to sleep and sealed the covenant Himself. That's huge; it means the weight of the promise didn't rest on Abraham or his descendants. God seemed to be saying, "I've got this. I'm committing to fulfill My word, period." But let's be clear: This doesn't mean Abraham's descendants could just live however they wanted without consequence. God's faithfulness never gave them a free pass; it gave them a secure foundation. They were still called to walk in obedience, or else they'd face correction, exile, and discipline (which history shows they did several times). The covenant was unconditional in promise, but not without expectation.

Okay, so here's where the reality-TV-show-worthy family drama starts happening. Abraham ends up with two sons: Ishmael (with his servant Hagar) and Isaac (with his wife, Sarah). Both are his biological kids, but God was super specific about which son would carry on the covenant. He told Abraham straight up, "It is through Isaac that your offspring will be reckoned" (Genesis 21:12 NIV). Paul backed this up later in Romans

9:7–9, making it clear that just being related to Abraham by blood wasn't enough to carry the covenant; you had to be part of the specific covenant line God chose.

Now, before anyone gets upset thinking God played favorites and left Ishmael out in the cold, that's not what happened. God blessed Ishmael big time and promised to make him and his descendants (traditionally understood as Arab peoples) into a great nation too (Genesis 17:20). And when we say *big time*, we mean it. Ishmael's descendants ended up settling in what is now a big part of the Arabian Peninsula (Genesis 25:18). How wild is the mercy and grace of God to still bless Ishmael and his descendants?

But let's pause for a moment and rabbit-hole. If you know about global resources at all, you're probably familiar with how rich in resources, oil especially, the Arabian Peninsula is. Could it be a result of the blessings of God stemming all the way back to a promise that He made to Ishmael? Are those nations reaping the benefits of an honest and just God? This would without a doubt be a *Faith and Friction*–worthy episode. Can you imagine the villain origin story that could come from Ishmael and his descendants that would allegedly result in an entirely different religious practice for millions of people? But for now, happy rabbit-holing! Let's get back to the topic at hand. Yes, God made a promise to bless Ishmael and his descendants, but the *covenant* promises? Those went through Isaac alone.

So Isaac grew up and had twin boys: Esau and Jacob. And once again, God picked one over the other, and this time it was Jacob. God was so invested in this guy that He even gave him a new name: Israel, which literally means "he who wrestles with God." (Pretty epic name, right?) Jacob/Israel then had twelve sons, and these twelve brothers became the founding fathers of the twelve tribes of Israel.

But wait, here's where the math gets a little funky and honestly kind of confusing. Jacob had twelve sons, but one of them, Joseph (yeah, the guy with the famous colorful coat), had two sons of his own: Ephraim and Manasseh. Jacob decided to adopt these grandsons as his own sons (Genesis 48:5–6). So technically, that makes thirteen tribal groups, but they still call them the "twelve tribes" because Joseph's name got swapped out for his two sons' in the official count. It's kind of like when a company reorganizes but keeps the same brand name.

When we're talking about Jewish people in the Bible, we're talking about descendants of Abraham, through Isaac, through Jacob/Israel. Think of it like a very specific family tree that God handpicked for His purposes. According to Scripture, Jewish identity comes down to bloodline, literally being descended from these specific guys whom God chose.

The Word *Jew*

So where does the word *Jew* come from? Originally, the term *Jew* came from "Judah," one of Jacob's twelve sons and the tribe that came from him. The tribe of Judah would become super important. King David came from this tribe, and eventually Jesus Himself did too. But to understand how all twelve tribes ended up being called *Jews*, we need to fast-forward through some pretty intense history.

Around 931 BC, because of King Solomon's mess-ups with idol worship, God allowed the united kingdom of Israel to split into two separate countries (1 Kings 11:11–13, 29–39): the Northern Kingdom of Israel (with ten tribes) and the Southern Kingdom of Judah (with the tribes of Judah and Benjamin, plus the Levites who worked in the temple). In 722 BC, the Assyrian Empire came in and completely conquered the Northern Kingdom. They deported the ten tribes and scattered them throughout their empire. These became known as the "Lost Tribes of Israel" because they basically vanished from history as distinct groups. The Southern Kingdom of Judah held out longer but eventually got conquered by Babylon in 586 BC. The difference was, after seventy years of exile, some of them actually came back home. The book of Ezra tells us exactly who returned: "Then rose up the heads of the fathers' houses of Judah and Benjamin, and the priests and the Levites" (1:5 ESV).

So from that point on, the Jewish people consisted mainly of three tribes: Judah, Benjamin, and Levi. Since Judah was the biggest and most prominent, all the tribes started being referred to as Jews. When people talk about Jews today, the thought is that they are primarily talking about descendants of these three surviving tribes.[2]

Fast-forward about two thousand years to the time of Jesus. The Jewish people were still there, still following their traditions, still waiting for the Messiah that God had promised. When Jesus showed up, He didn't look like what most people expected from a messiah. Instead of rolling up as a conquering king ready to throw down and kick out the Romans, He came as a carpenter from a small town, teaching about love, forgiveness, and a totally different kind of kingdom. This created a massive question for the Jewish people: "Is this who we've been waiting for?"

The Jewish community split into two groups:

- **Group 1:** Jews who said, "Yes! This is definitely our Messiah!" This included His twelve disciples (all Jewish), the apostle Paul (a hardcore Pharisee from the tribe of Benjamin), and thousands of other Jewish believers. These Jewish followers of Jesus actually carried the message to non-Jews despite facing intense persecution. They literally founded what we now call the church. We refer to this group as messianic Jews, because they believe that Jesus was in fact the Messiah.
- **Group 2:** Jews who said, "Nope, this isn't our messiah. We're still waiting." This group kept following traditional Jewish practices and beliefs. To this day they are still awaiting a messiah. They are most commonly referred to as Orthodox Jews.

Here's the key thing to remember: Both groups stayed Jewish. Believing in Jesus didn't make someone stop being Jewish any more than rejecting Jesus erased someone's Jewish heritage. They were still descendants of Abraham, Isaac, and Jacob from the tribes of Judah, Benjamin, and Levi.

Reconnecting the Dots

Are we feeling a little more confident in the backstory of God's promise and the Jewish people? On a serious note, we pray again that all of this would bring confidence to the conversation pertaining to biblical prophecy. And in this particular chapter, the Jewish people's involvement.

Most of us in the Western church have a complicated

relationship with the Jewish people and Israel. We know they exist, and we know they are mentioned in the Bible, but aside from the occasional Easter mention or *The Passion of the Christ* rewatch where the Jewish leaders nail Jesus to the cross, their story and their significance aren't really taught from many pulpits. They are like those distant relatives we all know we have but don't really talk to, or the ones who we don't really claim at all. They are often seamlessly grouped into the government, policies, and practices of the current nation as a whole. So when we are talking about the covenant-carrying descendants, we have to look to Scripture to address what it all means.

From the very beginning of redemptive history, God's relationship with the Jewish people has been marked by covenant, calling, and divine purpose. The church has been grafted into the root, not the other way around. Israel and the Jewish people are not sidelined in the story of God; they are central to it.

The connection between Jews and Christians has always been divinely woven. Paul wrote in Romans 1:16, "For I am not ashamed of the gospel of Christ, for it is the power of God to salvation for everyone who believes, for the Jew first and also for the Greek." Now, many of us growing up in the church never really had a sermon series talking about the Jewish people. But the history of Jews is so deep and so biblical. In a Western mentality, where we like to think we are the center of all that is happening, Paul humbles us and says, "Nope, the Jew first." He reminds us that Christianity didn't start with us; it started with the birth of the church in Acts 2 at Pentecost. Of

Israel and the Jewish people are not sidelined in the story of God; they are central to it.

all the people God could have chosen to transmit His message, He chose the Jewish people. Yet for centuries the Western church has treated the Jewish people like they were replaced instead of chosen. But what does "for the Jew first" really mean? Let's dig in a little more on that. If you don't already have it handy, get your Bible out, class. Let's go through some scripture.

CHAPTER 5

DOES ISRAEL STILL HAVE A SEAT AT THE TABLE?

The Plot Twist We May Have Forgotten About

The Bible is, first and foremost, a Jewish book. From Genesis to Revelation, its authors, culture, and language are deeply Jewish. All the New Testament writers, with the exception of Luke, were Jewish. Jesus Himself was a Jew, born from the tribe of Judah, descended from David. He boldly declared in John 4:22: "You worship what you do not know; we know what we worship, for salvation is of the Jews." Paul echoed this in Romans 1:16: "For I am not ashamed of the gospel of Christ, for it is the power of God to salvation for everyone who believes, for the Jew first and also for the Greek."

The phrase "Jew first" is not a temporal accident. This reflects a divine order, a redemptive sequence that honors the faithfulness of God to His promises. Jews hold a place of divine *priority*, not *superiority*, in God's plan, as highlighted throughout Scripture. In a message entitled "To the Jew First, and Also to the

Greek," pastor and author John Piper breaks down ways that the Jew, in fact, comes first.[1] Let's look more closely at these ways, using Piper's framework along with our own discoveries.

1. Chosen First: A People of Covenant

The Jewish people were chosen before the Gentiles to be God's chosen people. This choosing was not based on merit but on God's sovereign grace and promise. Genesis 12:1–3 recounts this promise. "Now the LORD said to Abram, 'Go from your country and your kindred and your father's house to the land that I will show you. And I will make of you a great nation, and I will bless you and make your name great, so that you will be a blessing. I will bless those who bless you, and him who dishonors you I will curse, and in you all the families of the earth shall be blessed'" (ESV).

God's covenant with Abraham, Isaac, and Jacob laid the foundation for everything that followed. Israel was essentially the womb through which the Messiah and the Word would come. The priority of the Jews is rooted in God's eternal promise.

2. Entrusted First: Guardians of God's Revelation—the Old Testament Scriptures

The Jews were the first recipients and stewards of God's Word. Paul acknowledged this explicitly in Romans 3:1–2: "What advantage then has the Jew, or what is the profit of circumcision? Much in every way! Chiefly because to them were committed the oracles of God."

The Scriptures, the very Word of God, were delivered through Jewish prophets, priests, and apostles. Without their faithfulness to preserve it, the world would not have access to the revelation of God.

3. Visited First: Jesus the Messiah Came to the Jews

Jesus did not arrive randomly. He came intentionally, as a Jew, to the Jews. Romans 9:5 says, "From [the Jews], according to the flesh, is the Christ, who is God over all, blessed forever. Amen" (ESV). Jesus was born of a Jewish mother, raised under the law, and ministered primarily to the Jewish people. His mission initially focused on them.

4. Salvation Flows Through the Jews

Now, this one is going to be a little longer, so strap in! We will explain the idea of salvation flowing through the Jews so it makes sense. Don't let the subtitle throw you off. Let's elaborate.

Again, Jesus' own words are key: "Salvation is of the Jews" (John 4:22). The divine seed, the lineage of the Messiah, was protected and preserved through the Jewish people. Abraham was not just the father of one nation but the channel through which all nations would be blessed. Galatians 3:7 tells us that through faith, believers become spiritual descendants of Abraham. That promise predates the Mosaic law and is fulfilled through faith, not nationality. Gentiles are grafted into Israel's covenant, not by replacement but by adoption.

Hang in there, this is about to be a lot of scripture! But the Bible paints such a great picture to help grasp all of this. In Romans 11:11–27 Paul says:

> Did God's people stumble and fall beyond recovery? Of course not! They were disobedient, so God made salvation available to the Gentiles. But he wanted his own people to become jealous and claim it for themselves. Now if the Gentiles were enriched because the people of Israel turned down God's offer of salvation, think how much greater a blessing the world will share when they finally accept it.
>
> I am saying all this especially for you Gentiles. God has appointed me as the apostle to the Gentiles. I stress this, for I want somehow to make the people of Israel jealous of what you Gentiles have, so I might save some of them. For since their rejection meant that God offered salvation to the rest of the world, their acceptance will be even more wonderful. It will be life for those who were dead! And since Abraham and the other patriarchs were holy, their descendants will also be holy—just as the entire batch of dough is holy because the portion given as an offering is holy. For if the roots of the tree are holy, the branches will be, too.
>
> But some of these branches from Abraham's tree—some of the people of Israel—have been broken off. And you Gentiles, who were branches from a wild olive tree, have been grafted in. So now you also receive the blessing God has promised Abraham and his children, sharing in the rich nourishment from the root of God's special olive tree.

But you must not brag about being grafted in to replace the branches that were broken off. You are just a branch, not the root.

"Well," you may say, "those branches were broken off to make room for me." Yes, but remember—those branches were broken off because they didn't believe in Christ, and you are there because you do believe. So don't think highly of yourself, but fear what could happen. For if God did not spare the original branches, he won't spare you either.

Notice how God is both kind and severe. He is severe toward those who disobeyed, but kind to you if you continue to trust in his kindness. But if you stop trusting, you also will be cut off. And if the people of Israel turn from their unbelief, they will be grafted in again, for God has the power to graft them back into the tree. You, by nature, were a branch cut from a wild olive tree. So if God was willing to do something contrary to nature by grafting you into his cultivated tree, he will be far more eager to graft the original branches back into the tree where they belong.

I want you to understand this mystery, dear brothers and sisters, so that you will not feel proud about yourselves. Some of the people of Israel have hard hearts, but this will last only until the full number of Gentiles comes to Christ. And so all Israel will be saved. As the Scriptures say,

"The one who rescues will come from Jerusalem,
and he will turn Israel away from ungodliness.
And this is my covenant with them,
that I will take away their sins." (NLT)

In these verses Paul lifts the veil on a divine mystery. The temporary hardening of Israel has a purpose. Their stumbling was not final; it was providential. Israel's rejection of the Messiah opened the door for the Gentiles, which is most of us, to receive salvation. If you're struggling to grasp all of this, you're not alone. This is one of those passages that can make your brain hurt a little, and that's okay. Paul himself calls it a *mystery* in verse 25, and then immediately explains *why* he's revealing it: "so that you will not feel proud about yourselves."

Think about that for a moment. God doesn't reveal mysteries to make us feel smart or superior. He reveals them to keep us humble. The mystery of God's ongoing faithfulness to Israel and the Jewish people can feel like a theological tension point, especially if you've been taught that the Church replaced Israel. But that tension? It's actually a gift. It's an invitation.

This is the perfect moment to slow down and invite the Holy Spirit to guide you. You don't have to figure it all out right now. You don't have to defend what you've always believed. Just ask, "God, help me understand this. Show me what You're saying. Keep my heart humble." Because the danger isn't in wrestling with mystery. The danger is in prideful certainty that dismisses what Scripture actually says. Don't rush past the discomfort. Let God meet you in the questions and guide you into understanding that doesn't lead to pride, but to humility and awe.

A Quick Time-Out for Clarity

Now, if you're like us, you may have a hard time grasping the idea that Israel's rejection could turn into our salvation. It truly is a mystery that we have the opportunity to invite the Holy Spirit to help us understand and navigate. Paul said in verse 25 of Romans 11, "I want you to understand this mystery, dear brothers and sisters, so that you will not feel proud about yourselves. Some of the people of Israel have hard hearts, but this will last only until the full number of Gentiles comes to Christ" (NLT). In the New King James Version, "hard hearts" is rendered as a "blindness." It's crazy to think about what a temporary hardening or blinding could even mean. Are there Jews, because of this blinding, literally unable to recognize or accept the truth of Jesus as the Messiah? Is this divine intervention for the sake of the Gentile? If this hardening hadn't taken place, would Jews be able to recognize Jesus? It's hard to say, and it's crazy to think about.

It reminds us of when Moses asked Pharaoh to let God's people go. Exodus 7:3 says that God was the one that hardened Pharaoh's heart. We don't know about you guys, but we've definitely had conversations as to why this might have been. Some argue that because Pharaoh's heart was already hard toward God's people, God just let it play out on its own. But others say it was a supernatural hardening that took place for the sake of fulfillment. Could this have been another one of those moments? What would have happened if God didn't harden Pharaoh's heart? Would he have let God's people go after the first plague? Or was there a greater purpose God was aiming for? (We have a podcast that touches on God's reason for the plagues that is amazing by the way.[2])

So if God's hardening of Pharaoh served a greater redemptive purpose, could the same be true here? Paul seems to think so. He shows us that even Israel's temporary blindness is part of God's master plan. Not to punish them, but to bring salvation to the whole world. Despite this hardening, Paul expressed that Jews were cut from the tree that we are grafted into. That Jews, who are from the original "tree," can be grafted back in. Paul explained that the salvation of the Gentiles was meant to stir Israel to jealousy, a holy longing to return to the God who had first chosen them. He called this fall of Israel "riches for the world" (v. 12), and he challenged the Gentiles not to become arrogant in their newfound inclusion. Imagine that! Gentiles are finally getting the invitation to the family reunion and the temptation to stir up drama is already there.

Paul used the metaphor of an olive tree to describe the relationship: Israel is the natural tree, rooted in covenant promises. Gentiles are the wild branches, grafted in by faith. Some of the natural branches (unbelieving Jews) were broken off, but not forever. God is still able, and willing, to graft them back in.

Paul warned Gentile believers not to boast against the natural branches. They don't support the root; the root supports them. He reminded them that if God did not spare the natural branches due to unbelief, He certainly will not spare arrogant Gentiles either.

That may still be a confusing concept to grasp. Let's explain it in a way that might be easier to understand. You don't have to choose between Michael Jordan or LeBron James to appreciate greatness (even though we know who the real GOAT is). One didn't cancel the other. Jordan changed the game. LeBron carried it forward. Different eras, with the same mission, elevate the game.

Now, imagine walking into a room full of basketball history, trophies, highlight reels, and legends. You weren't there for the incredible '90s dynasty that was the Chicago Bulls. You didn't witness the tongue-out drives, the midair switch-ups, or the six rings earned the hard way. But you benefit from it. You now know the culture. You rep the brand. You play the game because someone laid the groundwork.

That's kind of what Paul was getting at in Romans 11. He was warning Gentile believers, basically saying, "Hey, don't get cocky. You've been grafted in. You're part of this now, but you're not the origin story."

Think of it like this: Israel (the Jewish people) is Michael Jordan. The OG. The one who set the standard, fulfilled the prophecies, received the covenants, carried the weight of the law, and literally birthed the Messiah. The Jewish people are the ones God first revealed Himself to and through.

Gentile believers? We're the LeBron era. He may not be your favorite player, but journey with us for the sake of the analogy. LeBron has a new audience, new reach, global impact, but the same game. LeBron stands on the shoulders of those who came before him, like Michael Jordan. Similarly, we're standing on the shoulders of something sacred and ancient. We're part of the plan, but not the originators of it.

When Gentiles start acting like the church replaced Israel, like the new has fully erased the old, it's like saying LeBron made Jordan irrelevant. That's not just inaccurate; it's disrespectful to the legacy. Jordan made the league what it is. Without him, there is no platform for what came next. And guess what? Jordan and LeBron shouldn't be at odds. They're connected by the same story of greatness.

In the same way, the old covenant and the new aren't in competition. They're in *continuity*. God's promises to Israel weren't revoked; they're still unfolding. And the inclusion of the Gentiles isn't a plot twist; it's part of the plan from the beginning.

So don't boast against the natural branches. Don't act like God hit Delete on Israel and just Ctrl+P-ed a new plan with the church. This isn't a replacement story. It's a redemption story, and everyone gets a seat because of grace.

Time-Out Over: Back to the Game

To be honest, this whole concept could stop anyone in their tracks. Scripture explains this in detail, and it still creates conceptual tension for many. When Paul revealed the mystery of Israel's hardening, he suggested that it is partial and temporary. Not every Jewish person was "blinded," and it won't last forever. It will last only until the fullness of the Gentiles comes in, a prophetic benchmark in God's redemptive timeline. Once again, Israel's rejection of Jesus as the Messiah opened the door for the rest of the world to be invited into God's family. It created space for people from every nation and background to receive the gift of eternal life through Jesus.

Now, when Paul talked about "the fullness of the Gentiles," what exactly does that mean? Is it about every individual person on earth hearing the gospel? Is there a set number of people who have to say yes to Jesus? How exactly do we interpret that moment Jesus referred to in Matthew 24:14, where He said the gospel will be preached in all nations before the end comes? There are different interpretations here, and scholars have debated it for years. But here's what Paul was absolutely sure about: When that moment hits, something major is going down. He said with complete confidence that "all Israel will be saved" (Romans 11:26).

Does this mean that every Jew throughout history will be saved? Maybe, maybe not. But there will be a future collective turning of the Jewish people back to their Messiah. Paul cited the prophetic words in verses 26–27. Can you imagine what that'll look like?

God's covenant with Israel is not void. It's active, alive, and awaiting fulfillment. The story isn't over; it's unfolding. And the end will not merely be Gentiles brought in, but Jewish restoration. It isn't Gentiles instead of Jews; it'll be Gentiles *and* Jews. The church's posture should not be pride but prayerful humility, gratitude, and expectant intercession for the people God first called His own. This grafting into Israel's olive tree is not a transfer of ownership but a joining to the root. The Gentile church should not boast over Israel but pray for her fullness and restoration.

Whew! You made it to the end of that one. Hopefully you feel more confident in your understanding of salvation flowing through the Jews and what that means and looks like. And hopefully you recognize who the true basketball GOAT is.

5. Evangelized First: The Gospel Spreads

In the early church, Paul had a clear strategy: He went to the synagogue first in every city. Acts 13:46 records: "Then Paul and Barnabas answered them boldly: 'We had to speak the word of God to you first. Since you reject it and do not consider yourselves worthy of eternal life, we now turn to the Gentiles'" (NIV).

Even in his calling to the Gentiles, Paul kept the salvation of his own people close to heart. Romans 11:13–14 affirms: "I am talking to you Gentiles. Inasmuch as I am the apostle to the Gentiles, I take pride in my ministry in the hope that I may somehow arouse my own people to envy and save some of them" (NIV). In other words, Paul was saying that he wanted to make them jealous so that they might be saved. So even in his ministry to the Gentiles, one of Paul's goals was to get the Jewish people saved.

6. Blessed First: Recipients of Gentile Generosity

The early Gentile churches financially supported the Jewish believers in Jerusalem. Paul gave clear instruction for collections in 1 Corinthians 16: "Now concerning the collection for the saints, as I have given orders to the churches of Galatia, so you must do also . . . to bear your gift to Jerusalem" (vv. 1, 3). Romans 15 and 2 Corinthians 8–9 also show Paul viewing it as a spiritual duty.

Imagine being in a church or ministry staff meeting and you're deciding what the budget for missions is going to be. For Paul it would have undoubtedly been, and was, for Jerusalem and the Jewish people. He understood God's heart for His people. That heart was, and still is, one of covenant love and restoration. God chose Israel not as an afterthought but as the firstborn among the nations, set apart to carry His name and His promises. His heart has always been to draw them close, bless them, and through them, bless the world. Even when they stumbled, His desire never changed: to redeem, restore, and fulfill every word spoken to Abraham, Isaac, and Jacob. God's heart beats for relationship, and His covenant with Israel is a testimony that He is faithful to His word.

7. Judged and Rewarded First: Divine Accountability

Paul explained in Romans 2:9–10: "There will be trouble and calamity for everyone who keeps on doing what is evil—for the Jew first and also for the Gentile. But there will be glory and honor and peace from God for all who do good—for the Jew first and also for the Gentile" (NLT). The Jewish people were the first ones God chose to carry His message. They received the Law, the prophets, and the promises, and the Messiah came through their lineage. That's huge. But being first doesn't just automatically equate to blessings alone; it also means responsibility. Paul explained that "for the Jew first" comes with both the good and the hard.

Amos doesn't seem to sugarcoat this either. God basically says, "You're the only nation I revealed Myself to like this, so yeah, I'm holding you to a higher standard" (Amos 3:2, our paraphrase). Being chosen doesn't mean you get a pass; it means you're called to more. First in line for light or glory if they embrace the Messiah . . . and first in line for accountability.

A Divine Order, Not Favoritism

Being first does not mean being better. It simply means being first. Just like a firstborn child carries a certain honor and responsibility—especially in the times that Scripture was written—so also does Israel hold that place in God's plan. The other children are not less loved; they simply occupy a different role. Now we're sure that someone is reading this as the oldest child, or perhaps the youngest, and would beg to differ regarding that statement. Try to separate your understanding of favoritism in your house compared to God's house. This wasn't a matter of priority; it was just the order in which it all happened.

The Jewish people remain beloved (Romans 11:28). God's covenant with Abraham is eternal, and His gifts and calling are irrevocable (v. 29). The church has not replaced Israel; it has been joined to her story. Understanding Israel's role in God's redemptive timeline is not a matter of ethnic favoritism—it's a matter of biblical fidelity.

God made sure to highlight the importance of blessing Israel (Genesis 12:3; Numbers 24:9). They are the extended family coming back into the fold (Romans 11:25). Scripture alludes prophetically to a future time where all Israel will be saved and Christ will reveal Himself to the nation of Israel (Romans 11:26).

Israel wasn't a "starter nation" for God until He moved on to something better. In fact, the gospel message is not divided into "Only the Jews" or "Only the Gentiles." We as Christians are grafted into the fold, adopted into the family to receive all the blessings of Israel. Yet for many believers today, the Jewish people have faded into the background. This line of thinking has caused generational damage to the body of Christ and its perception of the Jewish people. In some cases, this had led to hatred toward the Jews, their customs, and their traditions, and has fed one of the biggest misconceptions—the idea of replacement theology, which is the belief that the Jews have been replaced by the church and there is no longer a "chosen people." This has become common within Westernized Christianity. Paul laid it out in Romans 3:23: "For all have sinned and fall short of the glory of God." That includes Jews. That includes Gentiles. That includes all of us. We all need the salvation that comes through Jesus. But it's important to understand Jewish history, and how it relates to God's plan.

There was a time not too long ago where the rise of the nation Israel in 1948 was celebrated as a significant prophetic event. A generation later, the heightening of tensions within Israel and the Middle East seem to present a problem for many believers. According to a recent study from the Center for the Study of the United States at Tel Aviv University, there has been an observable decline in support for Israel (68.9 percent in 2018 to only 33.6 percent in 2021) among the younger evangelical Christians.[3]

Why such a significant decline? Because we live in an era where social media shapes theology more than Scripture does. The modern narrative can often paint Israel in a negative light, or as an ultimate aggressor. Many equate what Israel's government partakes in as the voice and representation of biblically ethnic Jews. But this isn't just political. This is spiritual. So even with the understanding of "for the Jew first" and God's promises for Israel, we can see how God is moving in the Middle East as revivals are breaking out across the region. Does that mean that Israel is perfect, and the things that the government does line up with God's plan? Of course not. We recognize fully where that tension can be. And that tension can be extremely heavy and hard to process.

It seems as though one of the major goals of the Enemy has been to wipe out God's chosen people. First, he tried through Pharaoh in Egypt. Then through Haman in Persia. Then through Hitler in Nazi Germany. Now? It's happening through social media and in our schools. Could the battle against Israel for generations have been about coming against prophecy more than it's ever been about land? You have to admit, it is pretty crazy to think about all the global conflict that this tiny piece of land has caused throughout history. A piece of land comparable to the size of the state of New Jersey has been kept and preserved in more ways than one. There has to be something more to it.

Jesus was Jewish. He celebrated the Jewish feasts, taught in the synagogues, spoke the Jewish language, and had Jewish family. Of all the people groups Jesus could have chosen to descend from, He chose the Jewish people. He is coming back to the land of Israel. The Jewish people and Israel are of huge importance to believers. What happens with them are indicators of where on the road map of the end times we currently are and will be. The Jews have a purpose in God's divine timeline and plan. Once we understand that role, the purpose of a red cow, temples, the Antichrist, and everything in between can have its proper place in its significance to end-time prophecy. With that foundation laid, we can turn to what some think is one of the most pivotal pieces of prophecy still ahead: the construction of a new temple.

CHAPTER 6

WHY WOULD THERE BE A NEW TEMPLE IF WE ARE THE TEMPLE?

Salvation Doesn't Need a Temple. Prophecy Does.

We all crave a home—not just four walls and a roof, but a place where we're fully known and still fully welcomed. A place where the masks can come off, the striving can cease, and the ache in our chest finally eases. Deep down, we're all homesick for something this world can't quite offer. God knew this. He didn't just know it; He felt it too. Because from the very beginning, God wasn't looking for distance. He was looking for dwelling.

Enter: the temple.

He wanted a place to be with us. To restore what was lost in the garden. Not because He needed a house to live in, but because He wanted a place to dwell with us. A visible, physical space where we could, in a sense, touch heaven. A place where the eternal could collide with the earthly. So the Creator of the universe said in Exodus 25:8, "Make Me a sanctuary, that I may dwell among them." The temple wasn't just a holy site; the temple was God's address on earth. It mattered to Him. It mattered to the Jewish people too. So in this chapter we ask the question: Should it matter to us today?

Now, since you picked up this book, chances are your interest in end-time prophecy has already been piqued. If not, the topic of the Third Temple could be the spark in your journey, the plot twist you didn't see coming. Could the Scripture be pointing to something wild—another temple? A future temple that will stand in Jerusalem? We're talking about an actual, measurable, GPS–pin worthy temple on the Temple Mount.

Cue the goose bumps. Or maybe the questions.

Before we get into it, let's address some of the potential eye rolls and questions people are sure to have. We know, as believers, we are now the temple of God. And we'll talk about that more in a moment. The temple we believe Scripture is talking about isn't like the temples of the past. As believers we understand that because of Jesus and the cross, we no longer need a priest to go into the presence of God so our sins can be forgiven. The Holy Spirit now dwells in us. But this isn't about it being this *or* that. Rather it's this *and* that. It's the Spirit dwelling in us upon salvation, and the Third Temple for fulfillment of prophecy.

Let's read the fine print. Second Thessalonians 2:3–4 says, "Let no one deceive you by any means; for that Day will not come unless the falling away comes first, and the man of sin is revealed, the son of perdition, who opposes and exalts himself above all that is called God . . . so that he sits as God in the temple of God, showing himself that he is God." So we ask: How does the "man of sin" sit in the temple if there's no temple? Good question, right?

This is where it gets interesting.

We know from Scripture that believers are the temple of God (1 Corinthians 3:16–17). We're the spiritual house of God. In Ephesians 2 Paul expanded on this, saying the church is being built into a spiritual dwelling for God. It's like God moved from a one-location setup to a multicampus strategy, inside every believer. Referencing a temple isn't omitting the fact and truth that we are the dwelling place of the Spirit of God. But Scripture does allude to a physical temple coming in the last days. And you might be shocked by how the Bible refers to this temple.

In Matthew 24:15, Jesus spoke of the temple in physical terms, saying, "When you see the 'abomination of desolation' standing in the holy place... then let those who are in Judea flee to the mountains." Notice Jesus' use of the word *see*. That's not metaphorical. That's not "see it in your heart." That's "see it with your eyeballs." It's a location that's selfie-worthy (if that would even be allowed). It's a place you can stand in and say, "Whoa, this is happening!" (Sidenote: Jesus said, "when you see," meaning it's not there yet, but when it appears, that moment becomes a clear prophetic marker for the end times.) With this language surrounding these times we have to ask ourselves, *What is Jesus actually talking about here?* It isn't enough to just skip over the verse because we don't know. This seems to be too big of a clue to ignore. The tense used here is referring to a time yet to come to pass.

Another interesting detail: If you read 2 Thessalonians 2 carefully, you'll notice something you might find strange or unusual about the language. It doesn't call it the Antichrist's temple.

It doesn't call it the evil temple. Or the abomination place. No. It calls it the temple of God (v. 4). Now that's interesting, right? Why did Paul refer to this temple as God's? Even Jesus, in red letters, referred back to the book of Daniel and called it the "holy place" (Matthew 24:15). Jesus seems to have taken out the guesswork when He provided this detail.

Despite the dark drama that will unfold in this temple (you know . . . the guy who's not the Messiah but stands in the temple and says he is, in order to deceive the world), God still calls this temple His. It's like when your toddler discovers the location of the markers and completely trashes your favorite room. You don't love what happened there, but it's still your house. And that ownership matters, because God isn't done with His house. What the Antichrist defiles, God will restore. In fact, the book of Ezekiel gives us one of the most detailed temple visions in all of Scripture and points to a future where God's glory returns in full force.

Ezekiel was a prophet who wrote down his visions and revelations from the Lord. Many believe that these visions only had spiritual implications, not natural, physical ones. But let's investigate this thought further. His vision of the temple as the Lord's dwelling place, as recounted in chapter 43, could be more than a "spiritual temple" as some believe, because Ezekiel told us that when the Lord returns, His glory will fill the temple (vv. 4–5). He doesn't seem to mean this metaphorically but tangibly, powerfully, and gloriously. So yes! We are the spiritual temple of the Holy Spirit, and our salvation is sealed in Jesus. That's absolute truth. But—and this is important—that spiritual reality doesn't eliminate the prophetic reality of a physical temple. For many Christians, the idea stops at "we are the temple," and anything beyond that feels unnecessary or even contradictory.

But what if both are true? What if God can dwell in millions of believers *and* manifest His glory in a specific physical location? Scripture doesn't limit God's presence to one mode or one place. He's not either/or. He's both/and. He is God. He does multipresence flawlessly.

Hopefully that's enough to at least intrigue any Christian, at least curious ones like us, to dig into what these temples are all about. This chapter isn't here to give you just another Bible study. It's here to help you see and decode the potential messages found within the text: what the temple was; why it mattered then (and why it matters now); and what's about to go down again, possibly in our lifetime. Because understanding God's dwelling place isn't about just looking back with awe; it's about looking forward with eyes wide open, asking the Spirit of God to journey with you to bring the pieces together. And you're part of the story too!

Where Did the Whole Temple Thing Begin?

Okay, let's do a bit of a temple rewind. The OG tabernacle wasn't technically called a *temple*, but it was the first God-ordered holy dwelling. Think of it as the mobile-home version (not in look but in function) of God's house. The tabernacle, also called the Tent of Meeting, was a portable setup, kind of like the world's first pop-up church. Exodus 25–40 gives the specs. God wasn't winging this design; it was an actual divine blueprint with IKEA-level instructions (obviously way better, but who doesn't love IKEA?). The tabernacle was "a copy and shadow of what is in heaven" (Hebrews 8:5 NIV). If you ever wondered whether you could glimpse heaven, this was that glimpse—an accurate copy of heaven! One with specifications so precise, God said, "Make this tabernacle and all its furnishings exactly like the pattern I will show you" (Exodus 25:9 NIV). The tabernacle had an outer court (think: spiritual lobby), the Holy Place (VIP access), and the holy of holies (basically, heaven's throne room on earth). This Tent of Meeting traveled with the Israelites in the wilderness. It was God's way of saying, "I'm not just watching you from above. I'm walking with you."

Fast-forward to the time of King Solomon, son of David. Solomon got the green light to build the first permanent temple. And boy, he did *not* hold back. We're talking top-of-the-line everything: cedar from Lebanon, gold overlays, ornate carvings, the ark of the covenant rehomed in style (1 Kings 8:6–11). And speaking of style, Solomon carved two massive cherubim on the walls. What's *cherubim*, you may be asking? Think divine bodyguards straight out of a supernatural Marvel movie: *Guardians of the Garden*. These weren't your average chubby baby angels you often see in Renaissance art, cathedrals, and Valentine's Day decor. We're talking four faces (human, lion, ox, eagle), four wings, hands like a man under their wings, wheels within wheels covered in eyes, sparkling like burnished bronze; mysterious, majestic, fiery, and honestly, probably kind of terrifying. Their whole job? To guard God's presence, support His glory, protect sacred spaces like Eden, and lead some seriously epic worship in heaven. (See Ezekiel 1 and 10, Revelation 4:6–8, and Genesis 3:24 for the full mindblower.) Take a moment and count how many times you've heard a message or even podcast on cherubim. And people think the Bible is boring!

Now back to that ark. This wasn't just a sacred keepsake. It was the throne of God on earth, a holy hotspot where heaven and earth collided. It was placed between those larger-than-life Guardians of the Garden in the inner sanctuary, where God's glory showed up so intensely that priests couldn't even stand to minister (1 Kings 8:11). And while the ark vanished from the historical record after the First Temple was destroyed, whispers of it resurfacing still echo today, from dusty caves in Ethiopia to secret vaults in Jerusalem. Indiana Jones might've taken a swing at it, but scholars, adventurers, and even conspiracy theorists alike are still intrigued. Because when it does reappear? Game. Changer. That story would turn out to be better than any Indiana Jones or Nicolas Cage *National Treasure* movie, and history may have already pointed to it.

An Ancient Treasure Map? (Yes, Really)

What if we told you there's an ancient treasure map that might point to exactly where the ark of the covenant may be? Welcome to the wild, dusty world of the Copper Scroll. In 1952, in Qumran's Cave 3, just west of the Dead Sea and not far from the ruins of the Essene community that many believe were priestly caretakers of sacred temple artifacts, a scroll was found unlike any other. Most of the Dead Sea Scrolls were written on parchment or papyrus. But this one? It was engraved on copper, rolled up tightly like an ancient Fruit Roll-Up.

And its content? Not hymns. Not laws. Not prophecy. A list of treasure locations. I know, it actually sounds like the Bible meets *National Treasure*. But it's real. Over sixty locations are detailed, describing massive quantities of gold, silver, incense, and sacred vessels. Some scholars believe these are the hidden treasures of the First or Second Temple, possibly stashed away by priests fleeing the coming destruction. Others go even further. Could this scroll be pointing to the actual temple treasures of Solomon? Even the ark? Dr. Vendyl Jones[1] was a former pastor and biblical archaeologist who spent decades searching for the temple treasures, and some say may have even inspired the actual Indiana Jones character. He believed the Copper Scroll was written by priests trying to preserve temple artifacts ahead of the Roman invasion in AD 70.

Dr. Jim Barfield, a retired arson investigator, claims he's cracked the code of the Copper Scroll. His theory? The treasures are buried near Qumran in very specific locations, and he even believes the ark could be part of the stash.[2] Barfield's Copper Scroll Project has created buzz among prophecy circles and Israeli archaeologists alike. But digging in these spots? Not so simple. Politics, religion, and the explosive potential of unearthing sacred Jewish relics make it complicated. And yet, if he's right, it would be the biggest archaeological discovery in human history.

Here's another connection that might make your prophecy senses tingle. Dr. Jones also claimed that he found the previous red heifers' ashes near Qumran, the same desert region where the Dead Sea Scrolls were discovered. Some dismissed it as nothing more than desert soil and lye. But others couldn't help but wonder if he had stumbled onto something far more significant. Now, wouldn't that be crazy? History potentially connecting dots once again. All fueling the anticipation of a red heifer and new temple.

The Temple Institute, an organization in Israel dedicated to preparing for the rebuilding of the temple in Jerusalem, believes one of the red heifers found on the Texas ranch might be the final red heifer required to purify the Third Temple.[3] All of this traces back to that same mysterious, mountainous desert near Qumran. So if the Copper Scroll is real (and no serious scholar denies that it is), and if it really describes temple treasures (and a lot of people believe it does), then suddenly the idea of rebuilding the Third Temple stops being symbolic. It becomes active prophecy.

The Most Explosive Real Estate on Earth

This is why the Temple Mount remains one of the most explosive pieces of real estate in the world. The moment any excavation near Qumran, an archaeological site in Israel, turns up sacred Jewish relics, or worse (or better, depending on your view), the ark of the covenant, it would validate everything Scripture has said and threaten to blow up modern geopolitics. Temple Mount in Jerusalem is one of the most contested religious sites on the planet. It's already a flash point between Jews and Muslims. Now, throw the ark into the mix (yeah, the Ten-Commandment-tablet-holding, touch-it-and-you-might-die ark), the thing that would *require* Jewish access and possibly rebuilding of the temple. That's not just religious news. That's military-level, geopolitical, shake-the-world news.

Nations would pick sides. Radical groups would react. Prophecy-believers would see the end times rolling in. And for Israel, it wouldn't just be about spiritual destiny; it would become a battle of sovereignty, identity, and survival.

The ark returning would force every major religion, and every powerful government, to respond. Which is why even *talking* about it makes people nervous. So yeah, finding the ark wouldn't just shift faith conversations. It could redraw maps and rewrite history.

You think friction over global politics is intense now? Wait till the ark shows up. The Copper Scroll isn't just about ancient treasure; it's about prophetic confirmation. It's about a God who has preserved His covenant people, His sacred objects, and His promises across centuries of war, exile, and silence. It's about how faith often collides with fact, and how ancient secrets are waiting to be revealed in their appointed time. And it's about how the Third Temple isn't just a future hope; it may be closer than we think.

And Then Came the Wrecking Ball

So back to Solomon. Clearly he didn't just build a house. He built a holy magnet that hosted the very glory of God in a major way. But in 586 BC, Babylonian king Nebuchadnezzar came in like a wrecking ball. Solomon's masterpiece was destroyed, and Israel entered exile. Then came the weeping.

After exile, Persian king Cyrus pulled a surprise move. He let the Jews go home and rebuild. But why did he let them just go back? This is another example of God intervening for the sake of fulfillment of prophecy in Scripture. Ezra 1:1 says, "In the first year of Cyrus king of Persia, in order to fulfill the word of the LORD spoken by Jeremiah, the LORD moved the heart of Cyrus king of Persia to make a proclamation throughout his realm and also to put it in writing" (NIV). So not only did God move Cyrus's heart for the Jews to return, he said all their gold and silver was coming back as well. That same chapter reports 5,400 pieces brought with the exiles. Bowls, dishes, pans, all of the things. New fine china for everyone.

Here we find God, yet again, working on the hearts of people. For Pharaoh it was hardening. For the Jews it was blinding of the heart. And now we see Cyrus being moved in his heart. When you see these similarities in different parts of Scripture, it doesn't seem as random or far-fetched.

The Sequel That Missed Something Big

The next temple was Zerubbabel's, built under some serious opposition (Ezra 1–6; Haggai; Zechariah 4). According to Ezra, "Then the peoples around them set out to discourage the people of Judah and make them afraid to go on building. They bribed officials to work against them and frustrate their plans during the entire reign of Cyrus king of Persia and down to the reign of Darius king of Persia" (4:4–5 NIV). (Sidenote: Could this be a foreshadowing of what will take place in the building of the Third Temple?)

This temple wasn't as flashy as Solomon's, more like a fixer-upper, but it was still holy ground until Herod the Great (yes, the same one who tried to kill baby Jesus) later expanded and renovated it, making it one of the wonders of the ancient world. That's the temple Jesus walked into. The same temple that He flipped tables in. But here's the thing: Zerubbabel's temple didn't pack the same punch as Solomon's. The First Temple was loaded with God's glory, so heavy the priests couldn't even stand to minister. It had the ark of the covenant sitting in the holy of holies, representing God's throne on earth. When Babylon burned that temple down, the ark disappeared and was never replaced. According to ancient Jewish records, the Second Temple didn't have the ark, the mercy seat, or the visible glory of God. The presence that made Solomon's temple legendary? Gone. Cue the announcement: "Attention, everyone, the Lord has left the building." But in AD 70, Rome destroyed the Second Temple. Since then? No temple. Just a longing.

Now we're at the best part. One of the main questions, or at least the main point of tension and debate for many regarding end times conversation: Will there be a third temple? Remember, Orthodox Jews are still waiting for their messiah to come for the first time. That's why a physical temple matters so much to them. This temple isn't just symbolic. According to the Torah, they need it to offer sacrifices for sin, like it says in Leviticus and Deuteronomy. No temple, no sacrifices. No sacrifices, no atonement. And this isn't just fringe theory, folks. The Temple Institute has already prepared everything: the priestly garments, the instruments, even trained Levites ready to go. You can go to Jerusalem right now and see it all. Even crazier? Dr. Robert Mawire (we've mentioned him, right?) actually saw the blueprints for this future temple with his own eyes, handed to him by Prime Minister Benjamin Netanyahu.[4] Chaim Richman, a rabbi in Israel who was the executive director of The Temple Institute for more than thirty years, expressed that the Third Temple could be assembled in as little as four to six months.[5] Why so fast? Because, get this: The stones can be pre-carved and assembled off-site. In just the way 1 Kings 6:7 describes Solomon's temple, "No hammer or chisel or any iron tool was heard in the temple while it was being built."

So, what's the holdup? Right now, Temple Mount houses one of Islam's holiest sites. Building a Jewish temple there? Politically . . . complicated. But is it possible that the Jewish temple and the Dome of the Rock (a Muslim holy site on Temple Mount believed to be the place where Muhammad ascended into heaven), could actually coexist? On the same mount? At the same time? Sounds crazy, right? But Revelation 11:1–2 might actually back it up.

In this passage, John is told to measure the temple of God, but not all of it. God specifically says, "Leave out the court which is outside the temple, and do not measure it, for it has been given to the Gentiles." That detail is easy to gloss over, but it's huge. Why leave out the outer court? Because it's not under Jewish control. And guess what structure sits in the space believed by many to be the outer court? Yep, the Dome of the Rock.

Could this be more than just some modern speculation? Ezekiel's vision of the temple seems to possibly support this too. In Ezekiel 42:20, we're told that the outer wall of the temple was to separate what is holy from what is common. Other Bible translations, such as the King James Version, say that it will separate what is holy and what is "profane." That sounds a lot like a physical, geographical separation, not a symbolic one. This verse, along with the very literal, dimension-heavy descriptions in Ezekiel's temple vision, challenges the idea that the temple described is just a spiritual or metaphorical temple, as some scholars suggest. Ezekiel's temple had measurements, chambers, and gates, all mapped out in blueprints. It was tangible. Specific.

It's also important to question how, if this is referring to a spiritual or heavenly place as some might suggest, there could be a "profane" thing that the wall separates. If this is interpreted to understand that there is a profane place in, let's say, heaven, that opens up a whole additional conversation. The term *profane* in Ezekiel 42:20 refers to anything not set apart as holy. That could be unconsecrated people, places, or practices that are not fit for sacred use. The need to separate such things from the temple further confirms this is a physical temple on Earth, not a purely symbolic or heavenly one. Because in heaven, there would be no profane thing to exclude. Can you imagine finally getting to heaven, experiencing all of its beauty and splendor, and an angel comes up to you and says, "Hey, make sure you don't go over there to that unholy thing!" That'd be crazy, right? The Third Temple being an actual place definitely makes more sense when you start unpacking it. Still not convinced? Let's talk about the exact location.

Here's How It Could Actually Work

Dr. Christian Widener, a respected engineer and researcher, has done fascinating work on this.[6] Using biblical references, historical records, and archaeological data, he proposes that the original temple stood slightly north of the Dome of the Rock, right where the threshing floor purchased by King David was located. That's a key site. Second Chronicles 3:1 says Solomon began to build the temple "on Mount Moriah, where the LORD had appeared to his father David, at the place that David had prepared on the threshing floor of Ornan the Jebusite." That same threshing floor is also referenced in 2 Samuel 24:18–25 and 1 Chronicles 21:18–30, where David, after God sent judgment through plagues for his disobedience, built an altar for the atonement of his sin.

It's a place of sacrifice and divine encounter, a prophetic marker. Intriguingly, this ancient threshing floor is believed by many researchers, including Widener, to be located under what is now known as the "Dome of the Spirits," a small, unassuming structure on the northern end of the Temple Mount. This site aligns remarkably with the dimensions and placement of the original holy of holies, suggesting that the most sacred space in Jewish history may still be accessible and undisturbed!

Putting It All Together

So putting all of this together—the instructions in Revelation, Ezekiel's measured vision, and the historical location of the threshing floor—it starts to seem not only possible that a third temple could be built on the Temple Mount, but that Scripture may have hinted all along that it wouldn't have to displace the Dome of the Rock.

One of the most common objections to a literal fulfillment of Ezekiel's temple vision is the overwhelming size described in his prophecy. However, much of that scale comes from the large outer boundary meant to separate the holy from the profane, a perimeter that isn't part of the core temple structure itself. When that outer area is removed, what remains is a much more compact footprint consisting of the inner courts, altar, and the temple building. This scaled-down version, without the expansive outer wall, could realistically fit on today's Temple Mount and, as in Dr. Widener's theory, the holy of holies would sit directly over the Dome of the Spirits, a site believed by some to be the original location of the ark of the covenant.[7] This layout would avoid interfering with the Dome of the Rock or the Al-Aqsa Mosque, making it more feasible within modern political and religious boundaries.

You might be asking, "Why were these things built in the same spots to begin with?" In short, nothing in the Middle East is simple, and so many things are about sacred space.

Let's rewind.

CHAPTER 7

THE CLASH OF HOLY SITES

What Happens When Two Religions Claim the Same Ground?

The Temple Mount in Jerusalem is ground zero for biblical history. It's where Solomon built the First Temple, where the Second Temple stood, and where Jewish tradition says the Third Temple *must* be built. It's believed to be the exact spot where God's presence once filled the holy of holies.

But here's the twist: Hundreds of years after the Second Temple was destroyed by the Romans, Islam was born. And when Muslims gained control of Jerusalem in the seventh century, they built two holy sites *right on that same mountain*—the Dome of the Rock and the Al-Aqsa Mosque.

Why there? Well, it definitely wasn't random.

Muslims believe the prophet Muhammad ascended to heaven from that spot (called the Night Journey), so to them, it's the third holiest site in Islam. But to Jews? It's *still* the most sacred site on Earth.

So now you've got two massive world religions claiming the same patch of rock—and both say it's nonnegotiable.

The reason this matters for the Third Temple? The Jewish people can't rebuild it without that land. But removing or touching the Islamic sites would instantly trigger global outrage and possibly war.

So yes, it's *that* serious.

This isn't just real estate. It's prophecy, politics, and power all colliding on one little mountain in Jerusalem.

Wild, right? This doesn't seem to be just a matter of archaeology or politics; it's eschatology in real time. The friction on that mount reflects a deeper spiritual tension: the past and future colliding in a place where heaven once touched Earth . . . and just might again.

Jerusalem Recognized as the Capital, and What It Meant

Back in 2017, President Donald Trump did something that shook things up: He officially recognized Jerusalem as the capital of Israel. Now, that move wasn't just a nice gesture. It fulfilled the Jerusalem Embassy Act of 1995.[1] Israel has always considered Jerusalem its capital. Since 1949, its parliament (the Knesset), Supreme Court, and most government offices have been based in West Jerusalem. But because East Jerusalem is home to some of the most sacred sites in the world for Jews, Christians, and Muslims, and because Palestinians also hoped to claim it as their future capital, most countries have refused to officially recognize the whole city as Israel's capital. So instead, they kept embassies in Tel Aviv, trying to play neutral and avoid rocking the geopolitical boat. But in 1995, the United States passed the Jerusalem Embassy Act, a law that basically said Jerusalem was the capital of Israel and the US should move their embassy there. However, each president since 1995 exercised a waiver to delay it. Why? Because making that move could have stirred up a lot of tension in the Middle East. And no one wanted to be a part of opening that can of worms. So when President Trump recognized Jerusalem as the capital, it was a bold move. He began the process of moving the US Embassy from Tel Aviv. The embassy officially opened in the spring of 2018.

Why did this matter so much? Because in Middle East politics, symbolism is everything. Recognizing Jerusalem wasn't just about geography—it was about allegiance. The US was making a statement: We stand with Israel on this. Some countries praised the move; others condemned it, and protests erupted across the region. For Palestinians, it felt like a door was slammed shut on their hopes of claiming East Jerusalem as their future capital.

What seemed like a bold political decision to some may have carried much deeper prophetic weight. The world may have seen embassies and borders, but to those watching through the lens of biblical prophecy, it looked as if it could be another puzzle piece falling into place. That decision gave serious momentum to Jewish groups already pushing for the rebuilding of the Third Temple. Suddenly, Jerusalem wasn't just a dot on the map; it was front and center on the world stage, and a major world player gave not only backing but validity to the Jewish people of the nation. Some rabbis and Temple Mount activists began calling Trump a "Cyrus figure," kind of like King Cyrus in Isaiah 45, a Gentile leader God used to help rebuild the Second Temple.[2] They even minted gold coins with both Trump and Cyrus on them.[3] Which is kind of wild in and of itself. Now, we aren't saying to go gather and collect some Trump and Cyrus coins, but rather, to recognize how this may have moved the needle forward.

The way this came about may have been unexpected for mankind, but the reality of it remains. For a lot of people tracking end-time prophecy, this felt like a major green light. A clear sign that the conversation about the Third Temple isn't just for the distant future; it's something that could happen in our lifetime. That then opened the door for the Abraham Accords. The Abraham Accords were peace deals between Israel and a few major Arab nations that no one thought would happen in our lifetime. For decades, most Arab countries refused to make peace with Israel until the Israeli-Palestinian conflict was resolved. The idea was that until there was a Palestinian state, there wouldn't be peace. Then in 2020, everything seemed to flip. Under US mediation, Israel signed peace and normalization agreements with the United Arab Emirates, Bahrain, Sudan, and Morocco. These became known as the Abraham Accords, named after Abraham, the shared patriarch of Judaism, Christianity, and Islam.[4]

So what did the accords actually do?

- They opened diplomatic relations between Israel and these Arab nations.
- They allowed direct flights, embassies, trade deals, tech collabs, and tourism to flow and increase.
- They showed that peace with Israel didn't necessarily have to wait on a Palestinian agreement.[5]

That last part is what made it controversial. Although these Arab nations recognized the benefits of partnership with Israel, not everyone saw it as good. Supporters called it historic, a shift that could help stabilize the region and show that peace is possible. Critics, however, said that it sidelined the Palestinians and rearranged Middle East priorities for political and economic gain.

No matter where one stands, here's the friction point: The Abraham Accords reshaped the map. They shook long-held alliances and, at the same time, fulfilled some Bible prophecy watchers' expectations that nations would come into alignment before major end-time events.

Now, would we consider this to be peace in the Middle East? Not quite. But the Abraham Accords cracked open a door a lot of people thought may have been locked shut forever. Many believe these agreements could eventually create the kind of climate where Temple Mount discussions are even possible. Like, build-a-temple possible.

So here we are. Inching closer. Connecting the dots from our first red heifer encounter. Watching headlines. Reading prophecy not as distant predictions but as real-time checklists. And maybe you're wondering, *What does this have to do with me? I'm not a Jewish priest. I don't own a ram's horn. I can't even pronounce Zerubbabel.* But here's the thing: You're part of the story. Think about it. If we truly are entering into times that Scripture has foretold, what an honor it is to be the church during this time in history. That God would trust us to be the hands and feet of His body in this season and the seasons to come. It all becomes an opportunity to point people to the thing that truly matters the most: Jesus.

By having confidence in this conversation, we can point people right back to the main thing. But it's important to be able to also navigate the *now* things. The temple isn't just some ancient artifact; it's a prophetic signpost. It's not just about what was; it's about what is coming. Yes, you are the temple of the Holy Spirit. Yes, He lives in you. But let's not forget, He's still watching over that physical place in Jerusalem. And the moment that temple begins to rise again? It's not just symbolic; it's strategic. A signal. A shift. A fulfillment. Not one that is tethered to salvation or atonement for the believer in Christ, but one that is a major part in a story that is unfolding. That's why as believers, we can't afford to be passive or in the dark. God has given us prophetic intelligence, through His Word, not to scare us but to prepare us. So we won't be deceived. So we'll know the season that we're in. So we'll stand ready.

He's coming. And from what we are picking up from Scripture, the Third Temple is coming as well and will be ready. Will we? Let's stay awake. Let's keep reading. Let's be the watchmen on the wall.

This Is Holy Ground

So where exactly is the Third Temple supposed to go? And why is its location that important anyway? We talked a little bit about Temple Mount and its history earlier. But let's take a deeper dive into it. Mount Moriah, better known to many as the Temple Mount, is the original hotspot for Judaism, Christianity, and Islam. And trust us, it's way more than a scenic hill with a few old stones. It's a place dripping with history, prophecy, drama, and yes, a serious splash of political tension. So buckle up, this is gonna get good.

First, let's rewind back to one of the Bible's most iconic moments—the story of Abraham and Isaac. A little context: Did you know that Abraham is considered to be the grandfather of faith for Jews, Christians, and even Muslims alike? He's the starting point, the OG patriarch, for these three major world faiths. For Jews, he's the father of Isaac, through whom the Jewish people trace their lineage. For Christians, he's the blueprint of faith. Paul even called him the father of all who believe (Romans 4:11). And for Muslims, he's honored as a prophet and the father of Ishmael, who many Muslims believe is the ancestor of the Arab peoples and from whose lineage came the prophet Muhammad. All three religions look to Abraham as someone who walked with God, obeyed Him, and trusted Him even when it didn't make the most sense. So he's not just a historical figure. His story shapes billions of lives to this day.

Well, God asked him to take his son Isaac (or Ishmael in the Islamic tradition, cue a future *Faith and Friction* episode) up to this very mountain and sacrifice him (Genesis 22). Talk about a test, right? Abraham was ready to obey with no hesitation, but just in the nick of time, God provided a ram for the sacrifice instead.

This moment isn't just a story about faith and obedience; it's the foundational event that put Mount Moriah on the map for Jewish people. That moment wasn't just intense Old Testament drama; it was prophetic foreshadowing of the Father who would one day offer up His Son. This place has always been sacred real estate. For Jews, it's the holiest site on Earth. The place where their previous temples stood. Where the manifested presence of God dwelt. For Muslims, it's the location of the Al-Aqsa Mosque, one of the three holiest sites in Islam. And for Christians, it serves as a prophetic compass for things to come. It's more than just an ancient site; it's a spiritual epicenter with past, present, and future meaning for believers.

Now, here's where it gets a little dicey. Jews believe that the temple must be rebuilt to fulfill messianic prophecy. They aren't waiting for Jesus to return; they're waiting for a messiah to come for the first time. And the temple? That's a key part of his arrival. Many Christians believe the rebuilding of the temple is only necessary as a step in the return of Jesus, as hinted in Matthew 24 and 2 Thessalonians 2. Muslims oppose the rebuilding of the Jewish temple on the Temple Mount because the site is currently under Islamic control and houses the Dome of the Rock and Al-Aqsa Mosque. To them, the Third Temple isn't just a theological threat; it's a political and territorial one that can't be overstated. Hence the CBS article we mentioned in the beginning of this book.

So who owns the Temple Mount? Is there a title deed of this land out there somewhere that can settle any disputes? We did some research and what we discovered might surprise you. Assuming this all wasn't crazy enough, before 1967, East Jerusalem was controlled by Jordan. Not Palestine. Not Israel. Jordan took over the area, including the Old City and Temple Mount, after the 1948 Arab-Israeli War.[6] From 1948 to 1967, Jews weren't even allowed into East Jerusalem, including their holiest site, the Western Wall. It was a hard no.

But then the Six-Day War in 1967 happened. Israel launched a defensive strike, preempting several Arab nations gearing up to attack, and ended up taking back East Jerusalem (including Temple Mount). But after Israel captured East Jerusalem, they did something that seemed a little shocking. They gave administrative control of the Temple Mount back to the Islamic Waqf, a Muslim religious trust based in Jordan.[7]

But why?

Because Israel knew this land was a powder keg. So to avoid igniting an all-out religious war, Israel kept sovereignty but let the Waqf manage day-to-day affairs on the Mount.[8]

Translation: It's Israeli territory but with an Islamic landlord. And yes, it's as complicated as it sounds. "We control the land, but you manage the site." It was a peacekeeping move, or at least an attempt at one. There's an uneasy status-quo agreement in place, which basically means no non-Muslim prayer allowed on the mount. If you walk in with a Bible and start praying, that'll likely get you escorted out faster than you can say "shalom." This arrangement keeps things calm-ish, but tensions are always simmering.[9]

One question that has come up is, "Why can't the Jewish people get another piece of land and build the temple there?" Well, the Temple Mount is believed to be the exact spot where both the First and Second Temples stood. So for Jewish people, if a third temple is ever built, it's got to happen right here. This is the location that God chose for His temple.

In 1 Chronicles 21–22 we see David mess up big time (go check out those chapters to read the full story). Satan rose up against Israel and incited David to take a census of Israel (1 Chronicles 21:1). God's response? A plague. Sounds a bit harsh, right? But this census wasn't just an innocent headcount. David wanted to know how many fighting men there were in Israel. This was a shift in David from trusting the strength of God to trusting the strength of human numbers. David had a moment of misplaced security, and it cost him. But then something powerful happens in 1 Chronicles 21:18: "Therefore, the angel of the Lord commanded Gad to say to David that David should go and erect an altar to the Lord on the threshing floor of Ornan the Jebusite." That exact spot, Ornan's threshing floor, is what became the Temple Mount. David ended up buying the land and building an altar, and the plague stopped. Then in 1 Chronicles 22:1, David declared, "The house of the Lord God is to be here, and also the altar of burnt offering for Israel" (NIV).

David was told to build on that exact spot. Not just anywhere. And if you fast-forward a tad, you'll learn that David didn't build the temple himself because God said his hands had shed too much blood (1 Chronicles 28:3). But he gathered all the materials, got the blueprints straight from God, and passed them on to Solomon. And Solomon built the First Temple on that exact land: Mount Moriah, aka the Temple Mount. "Then Solomon began to build the temple of the Lord in Jerusalem on Mount Moriah, where the Lord had appeared to his father David. It was on the threshing floor of Araunah [Ornan] the Jebusite" (2 Chronicles 3:1 NIV).

Well, there we have it. There is a biblical basis that says this specific mountain is where the temple must go. There is something about this specific place that carries immense value. It appears to be more than just mere geography. It is holy ground, layered with covenant and destiny.

Real Estate, Rituals, and Some Wild Prophecies

This isn't just one of those "maybe someday" prophecies people talk about over coffee and conspiracy videos. Nope, there are actual groups out there putting boots on the (very sacred) ground to prepare for the Third Temple. One of them is a Jewish organization called Boneh Israel,[10] and get this: They went full real-estate-mogul mode and bought land on the Mount of Olives. Yes, that Mount of Olives. Where Jesus taught, walked, and prayed. The one with a direct line of sight to the Temple Mount. That Mount of Olives.

That land had been under Muslim control for centuries. Centuries! And then *boom*, along came Rabbi Yitshak Mamo, the global team lead at Boneh Israel, pulling a move that felt part Indiana Jones, part "spiritual real estate agent." It was like reclaiming your childhood home after years of it being in someone else's hands. That's how significant this feels for many—only it's way more prophetic.

About twelve years ago, Rabbi Mamo connected with a group called Uvne Yerushalayim (we would have skipped the pronunciation attempt too), a group that focuses on preserving Jewish history and educating the next generation, to secure this exact plot. Why this spot? Because, wait for it: It directly faces the original location of the holy of holies. Rabbi Mamo explained it had to be precisely aligned so that when the red heifer ritual goes down, the priest can literally see Temple Mount from where he's standing.[11] According to the Mishnah Parah (3:6–9), the line of sight during this ritual was important for the believed continuity it represented with where the presence of God was. For the Jewish people, it means that though the ritual takes place outside of Temple Mount, it's still spiritually connected. Talk about needing perfect GPS coordinates. The Mount of Olives was the exact place where the red heifer sacrifice happened during the Second Temple period. So all of this is not just symbolic. It's strategic, it's sacred, and it's got a whole lot of ancient-meets-modern prophecy energy.[12]

Speaking of prophecy that feels like it walked straight out of a Netflix political thriller, enter Dr. Robert Mawire again. We've spoken about him a couple of times already—Zimbabwean-born, Texas-based, Christian minister and prophetic voice to world leaders. Back in the early 2000s, Dr. Mawire dropped some serious prophetic truth bombs on not one but two Israeli prime ministers. First up: Ariel Sharon. Dr. Mawire warned him, straight up, that if he gave away Jewish land in exchange for peace, it would cost him both his leadership and his life.[13] Fast-forward to 2005. Sharon ignored the prophecy and pulled Israeli settlements out of the region. People are unsure as to why he did this. Maybe it was political pressure. But less than a year later, in January 2006, he suffered a massive stroke and slipped into a coma. He never recovered, eventually passing away because of it.

Now jump back to 2001, where Dr. Mawire sat across from Benjamin Netanyahu, who at the time was no longer prime minister and was in such serious political heat that it looked like he'd never recover. In 1996 Netanyahu became the youngest prime minister in Israel's history, a bold, right-leaning leader during a tense time of peace talks and terror attacks. But by 1999, the public had had enough. He lost reelection because he was seen as too hard-line for the peace process. The media dragged him. And his own party (Likud) was divided. By 2001, he was out of office and out of favor.[14] But things would take a turn for him.

Dr. Mawire told Netanyahu (probably not over coffee, but let's pretend), "God's not done with you. You'll be prime minister again, but don't ever negotiate land for peace."[15] Honestly, it sounds like a line from a spy film, but this really happened.

At the time, that sounded highly unlikely. Netanyahu was considered politically dead in the water by many. But wouldn't you know it, Netanyahu returned to power in 2009 and held on to it for more than a decade, during some of Israel's most intense geopolitical moments. Coincidence? Maybe. Or maybe it's what Dr. Mawire calls *prophetic intelligence*—a divine heads-up—not political advice. Either way, it's one of those moments where faith, politics, and prophecy intersect, like, "Wait . . . did God just speak into a cabinet meeting?" Because if He did, that's a whole different level of Middle East peace talks.

It can make you wonder a bit. What does God intervening in things like this look like? We see it happen in Scripture, but what does that look like today?

God still speaks. He speaks through His Word, through His Spirit, and even through people. He can still speak about real estate. About borders. About land. Because it's not just land. It's legacy. It's prophetic fulfillment. It's part of His unfolding plan.

Which brings us back to you. And your friend who still thinks Revelation is just Christian sci-fi. As believers, we need to be on the front lines of understanding prophetic timelines. Not to stockpile canned goods and move to a bunker (unless the Lord tells you to, in which case . . . pack snacks), but so we are not deceived. Let's not be the generation that memorizes TikTok dances but misses the signs of the times. Let's be the ones who

Let's not be the generation that memorizes TikTok dances but misses the signs of the times. Let's be the ones who carry prophetic intelligence, who study the Scriptures and the news together, not to panic but to prepare.

carry prophetic intelligence, who study the Scriptures and the news together, not to panic but to prepare.

God is moving. The temple is on the radar. The chessboard of nations is shifting. The Abraham Accords aren't just political flexing; they're puzzle pieces in a larger prophetic picture. Peace in the region might be what opens the door for the temple's rebuilding. And once the red heifer is sacrificed and that temple goes up? Buckle up. Because prophecy won't be slowing down after that.

CHAPTER 8

DOES DANIEL'S PROPHECY HOLD THE KEY FOR THE LAST DAYS?

The Code That Time-Stamped the Cross and Cues the End

The Bible is full of prophecy, and if you start tallying up all the prophecies Jesus fulfilled, it might just blow your mind. From where he was born (Micah 5:2), to how he rode into Jerusalem on a donkey (Zechariah 9:9), to even His royal lineage (Jeremiah 23:5–6), the numbers don't even sound real. Prophecies about Jesus are woven throughout Scripture, even places you may not expect. But before the talk of a third temple, an Antichrist, a mark, or a global meltdown, there was a timeline. Some people call it Daniel's prophetic timeline. You may have heard it called the "seventy-week prophecy" (we'll get to that more here soon). It's like the scaffolding the rest of the Bible is built on. It's where we get the structure for the tribulation, that period of time Jesus talks about in Matthew 24 where things are going to get real, real bad. The book of Daniel speaks about the timing of the Messiah's arrival and crucifixion, and the countdown to everything that's still ahead. It's how we're able to look back in order to look forward with anticipation.

Have you ever received a word from someone in a church or service setting? You know, the moment someone comes up to you, known or unknown, and they tell you, "I think the Lord has a word for you." A lot of times that goes one of two ways. Someone can actually give you an accurate prophetic word that not only resonates in the deepest way but changes things for you forever. Things no one else could have known. Things you've never spoken about out loud. In those moments you know it was from the Lord. It becomes a word that when you look back on your story, you can assess and pinpoint the impact it had. On the other hand, you may experience something totally different. You get that person who makes you a little nervous as they approach you. You brace yourself, remaining open-minded to what they might say. The Lord can use anybody, right? And then they absolutely bomb it. What they say has nothing to do with your life and doesn't resonate at all. And sometimes they're so far off base that the opposite is actually true. You sit there with a forced half smile wishing it would be over. Some of us have definitely been there.

Hypothetically of course, if you experienced both of those scenarios, which person would you trust to prophetically speak into your life again? If you said the latter experience, God bless you. We're not above second chances here. But obviously we're going with the one who got it right the first time. There would be a level of trust and confidence in their words because you've seen it play out the way they said before. This is the concept or idea we'll explore in this chapter. It's time to talk about one of the wildest prophetic books in the Bible: Daniel. This book is packed with visions, timelines, and prophecies that help us identify the dominoes that will fall before the second coming of Jesus Christ. But what if this wasn't Daniel's first rodeo? What if Daniel had prophetic insight on when Jesus was going to come the first time? And, wait for it . . . hundreds of years in advance. Scripture may be revealing just that. Let's get into it!

Math Avengers, Assemble

If you're a numbers person or secretly geek out over timelines, patterns, or biblical math, this is your chapter. There have been other places throughout this book where there were different number observations that felt too good to be a coincidence, but this is going to go even further. This is less of a "wow" chapter and more of a "whoa, everything connects" chapter. If the Antichrist is the villain, and the tribulation is the battlefield, then Daniel's timeline is the script God handed out long before the curtain ever rose. Understanding it doesn't just help you follow the story; it proves the Author knew the ending from the beginning.

So why does this matter for us today? Because the same prophetic clock that counted down to the cross is still ticking toward the return of Christ. If God's timeline for Jesus' first coming was this precise, you can trust He's just as precise about His second coming.

Understanding Daniel's prophecy isn't about trivia or spiritual math; it's about confidence. It's about living ready in a world that feels increasingly uncertain. If God could orchestrate world empires, kings, and calendars to the exact year for Jesus' first arrival, then nothing surprises Him. His timing is exact and every detail matters. That means He is in control of how all of this will end, and that truth should change how we live now.

In Luke 19:41–44 we see Jesus weep over the city of Jerusalem. He wept because they had everything they needed to recognize the times. The prophecies, the patterns, even the literal person of the Messiah, and they still missed it. They missed the visitation of the Messiah and the opportunity to be prepared spiritually. Today, we face a similar situation. It seems that we have what we need right now as well. We have the Word of God and its prophetic revelation, along with the Spirit of God and His discernment. It's all there; let's not miss it.

The Prophetic Blueprint

More than five hundred years before Jesus was born, God gave the prophet Daniel a divine timeline, down to what may have been the year of the Messiah's arrival and when He would die. This wasn't just a vague vision or cryptic code. It was a countdown: precise, mathematical, and seemingly undeniable. At the end of that prophetic download, Daniel was told something interesting, "Go your way, Daniel, because the words are rolled up and sealed until the time of the end" (12:9 NIV).

It seems that the blueprint for the events that would unfold leading up to the second coming of Christ have been there the whole time. Hidden in plain sight. A divine timeline that has been hidden for centuries, waiting for a generation ready to see it (Daniel 12:4, 9). Understand that God never winged any of this.

He wrote it all down, long before it happened, and invited us to pay attention.

A Week Isn't Always a Week (Welcome to Biblical Math)

Okay, deep breath. We're about to jump into one of what we believe may be the most mind-blowing, math-heavy, Bible-prophecy mic drops ever recorded. That may sound like a massive claim, but as we started digging more into the book of Daniel and ancient history, this puzzle just kept unfolding. Let's jump into some Scripture.

In Daniel 9:25–26, Gabriel says:

> "Know therefore and understand that from the going out of the word to restore and build Jerusalem to the coming of an anointed one, a prince, there shall be seven weeks. And for sixty-two weeks it shall be built again with squares and moat, but in a troubled time. And after the sixty-two weeks, an anointed one shall be cut off and shall have nothing. And the people of the prince who is to come shall destroy the city and the sanctuary. Its end shall come with a flood, and to the end there shall be war. Desolations are decreed." (ESV)

Let's break some of this down! So, the word *weeks* here is *shabuwah*, which literally means "sevens" or a "group of sevens."[1] Not seven days but seven-year periods. It's rooted in the biblical Shemitah cycle. A Shemitah cycle is where every seventh year was a Sabbath year for the land, and every forty-ninth year rolled into a Jubilee, when debts were canceled and captives were set free. The Shemitah cycle, introduced in Leviticus 25 and echoed in Deuteronomy 15, wasn't just about resting the land or forgiving debts. It established a God-ordained rhythm of time. This seven-year pattern became the foundation for how prophetic time is measured in Scripture, especially in the book of Daniel. How cool is it that God's calendar doesn't tick by in minutes and months; rather it moves in cycles of redemption?

When Gabriel talked about seven weeks and sixty-two weeks in Daniel 9, he was talking about sixty-nine sets of seven years, which equals 483 years total. If you need to take a moment and grab your calculator and notepad, now is the time. We've got more numbers coming your way and you're going to want to keep track! According to Daniel, the countdown to the Messiah's death would start with a decree to rebuild Jerusalem. That decree was given by the Persian king Artaxerxes in 444 BC (Nehemiah 2:1–8).[2] The first seven weeks (49 years) cover the actual rebuilding of Jerusalem's walls and infrastructure and finished around 395 BC. Then another sixty-two weeks (434 years) tick forward, bringing us to a key prophetic moment: the Messiah being "cut off."

Some of you with your TI-89 calculators just got offended by our calculations. This part is easy to miss but crucial: The math only works if you're using the prophetic calendar.

Unlike our solar-based calendar (365.25 days per year), the Bible often uses a 360-day prophetic year. Scholars refer to this as the "prophetic year," a consistent 360-day cycle used for calculating end times events and messianic prophecies.[3]

We know that sounds kind of weird, but it's not random. That time frame shows up consistently in both Daniel and Revelation, where 1,260 days = 42 months = 3½ years (Daniel

7:25, 12:7; Revelation 11:2–3, 12:6, 12:14). That's exactly 30 days per month and 360 days per year. You see this partially played out in Genesis with the flood as well. Scripture says the flood began on the seventeenth day of the second month (7:11) and ended on the seventeenth day of the seventh month, and it lasted 150 days (7:24, 8:3). One hundred and fifty divided by five equals 30 days. So if you're going on a twelve-month cycle, once again you get 30 days per month.

So let's do some prophetic math:

69 weeks of years = 483 years
483 years × 360 days = 173,880 days

Now fast-forward 173,880 days from Artaxerxes' decree in 444 BC, and you land squarely in AD 33. Are you tracking with us? Could this have been *the* week Jesus rode into Jerusalem on a donkey, hailed as King Jesus? And just days later was "cut off," or crucified? What?!

This doesn't just seem to be guesswork. This is God's prophetic calendar. Just a quick reminder, this was five-hundred-plus years before Jesus was crucified. Daniel wasn't throwing out mysterious numbers for fun; he was documenting a divine timeline that pointed directly to Jesus.

Was Jesus Really Thirty-Three?

Some people often speculate about Jesus' exact age when He died. Some say He was thirty, others say thirty-three, and some are even convinced He's secretly timeless. So let's continue digging through the numbers so that we can show you why thirty-three seems to be the age that fits prophecy perfectly.

Many historians now believe Jesus was born sometime in late 3 BC. That's because newer research suggests Herod the Great, who famously tried to kill the infant Jesus, actually died in early 1 BC, not 4 BC as earlier scholars thought.[4] This updated timeline makes a lot more sense when you look at all the historical details and fits well with the events recorded in the Gospels, like the visit of the wise men, the massacre of the innocents, and the family's flight into Egypt.

At first glance, it might seem tricky to line up that birth date with Jesus' crucifixion in AD 33, but once you understand how our calendar works, it all clicks into place. Here's the thing: Our modern calendar skips straight from 1 BC to AD 1. There's no "year zero" in between. So when you do the math from late 3 BC to AD 33, it adds up to about thirty-five years. But since Jesus was born near the end of 3 BC and crucified early in AD 33, that means He would have been roughly thirty-three years old at the time of His death. That lines up perfectly with Luke's note that He was "about thirty" when He began His ministry (3:23), and it fits with the common belief that His public ministry lasted around three to three-and-a-half years.

When you take all these pieces together—the revised dates, the calendar quirks, and the Gospel accounts—this 3 BC to AD 33 timeline doesn't just fit Daniel's prophecy; it fulfills it. It's like the ultimate prophetic puzzle where every piece falls into place exactly as predicted, showing us just how detailed and trustworthy God's Word really is.

For our math and number nerds, we hope you enjoyed digging into that. For those of you who are still spinning internally and going back over your math with your calculators, feel free to take a moment if necessary. And for those of you who just flat-out skipped it, I'm sure you're not alone. Deep breath. Let's keep going!

A Warning from the Temple

Daniel 9:26 continues: "And the people of the prince who is to come shall destroy the city and the sanctuary." That prophecy came true in AD 70, when the Roman general Titus led a brutal assault on Jerusalem and completely destroyed the Second Temple. But Daniel made something crystal clear: The Messiah had to die before that happened. And Jesus did.

If you were a first-century Jew searching the Scriptures and waiting for the Messiah, Daniel's prophecy would've given you a major clue: The Messiah had to be "cut off" before the temple fell. That narrows the window down dramatically. Which begs the question, If the temple fell and the Messiah had to be cut off, how come there are Jews who still think the Messiah hasn't come? Can this be the "sealed up to the end" we were talking about earlier? Or the blindness Paul was talking about (Romans 11:25)? It's often hard to comprehend supernatural occurrences of this nature in modern times. If someone could just make an epic Marvel-level movie of some of the things in this book, I'm sure a lot of us would appreciate it. Make it make sense!

Here's where it gets even more interesting. According to the Talmud, a book of discussions from Jewish rabbis and interpretations of Jewish law, something really wild used to happen every Yom Kippur, also known as the Day of Atonement. This was (and still is) the holiest day of the year for the Jewish people, a sacred time set aside for repentance and seeking forgiveness from God. It was the one day each year when the high priest would enter the holy of holies in the temple to make atonement for the sins of the nation.

Part of the ceremony (described in Leviticus 16) involved two goats. One of the goats would be sacrificed to the Lord, and the other would become the "scapegoat." The high priest would symbolically place the sins of the nation onto the scapegoat by laying hands on its head. They would send it out into the wilderness as a visual and representation of sin being carried away from the people. A strip of crimson wool would be tied to the scapegoat's head, and another piece tied to the temple door. According to tradition, if God accepted their repentance and forgave their sins, the crimson wool would miraculously turn white, which they believed was the fulfillment of Isaiah 1:18: "Though your sins are like scarlet, they shall be white as snow." Imagine standing there watching red turn to white before your eyes. How awesome would that be? Half the crowd's probably thinking, *Miracle*; the other half is yelling, "Witchcraft! AI! Deepfake!" Classic.

But then something changed. The Talmud (Yoma 39b) records that during the last forty years before the destruction of the Temple . . . the crimson-colored strap stopped turning white![5] According to Jewish tradition, this was a visible sign that God had not accepted the sacrifice and that the people's sins were no longer being forgiven as before.

So, to rewind, forty years before the temple was destroyed was around AD 30. That's when these signs just . . . stopped. The scarlet wool stopped turning white. The temple light went out. The doors opened on their own. And the presence of God, it seemed, had left the building.

Just think about that! Around the same time Jesus began His public ministry in AD 30, these eerie signs started showing up, like flashing neon signals from heaven that something big had shifted.

It was as if God was shouting from heaven: "Pay attention! Something greater is here!" Then in AD 33, Jesus, the true Passover Lamb, was crucified. The veil in the temple was torn. The final sacrifice was made. The system was fulfilled. And heaven made it loud and clear: The old was over. The new had come. But tragically, most of Israel missed it. The presence departed, and they didn't even realize He was already among them.

What Happens Next?

So, what's still on the prophetic clock? The Bible says the Third Temple will be rebuilt, and sacrifices will start up again. (Remember, though: The Jewish people can't just jump back into that without a very specific and ancient ritual—the purification ceremony of one of the main characters of this book, the red heifer.)

Daniel 9:27 drops us into what many call the final countdown: "He shall confirm a covenant with many for one week; but in the middle of the week he shall bring an end to sacrifice and offering." That "week"? That's the infamous seventieth week of Daniel, a.k.a. the tribulation. Which we know from all the fun math we did earlier that the "week" here is the same prophetic 360-day year in Daniel.

And that mysterious "he"? That's the Antichrist. The villain of all villains. He's going to broker a deal at the beginning of that seven years that looks like peace. A global sigh of relief. It will be the moment that opens the door for Jewish worship to start again in the rebuilt temple. But halfway through those seven years (at the three-and-a-half-year mark), he seems to flip the script. Mask off. Peace deal shredded.

He'll shut down the Jews' sacrifices and do the unthinkable: desecrate the temple and claim to be God. As much as this sounds like an actual movie that would undoubtedly be Oscar-worthy, this isn't fiction. This is where the Bible says the world is headed. And this is why prophecy isn't just interesting; it's urgent.

Will You Be Ready?

Here's the bottom line. It all started with a prophecy in the book of Daniel and it all leads back to this one unshakable truth: Jesus is the Messiah and He arrived right on schedule.

But here's what most people miss. That same prophetic clock? It's still ticking. It's why Jesus didn't say, "Chill." He said, "Watch." Because the clock didn't stop at the cross. And just like the first time, the second time won't be off by a minute. He's coming again, precisely on time. Not a day early. Not a second late.

The signs? They're stacking up. The patterns? Starting to repeat. The setup? Almost complete. The question isn't if He'll return. The real question is: Will we be ready when the clock strikes again?

In the next chapters, as we continue following the prophetic thread from Daniel, we will step into the territory many of you have probably been waiting for. This is where the conversations often heat up. Where curiosity spikes and theories tend to run wild. We're talking about the Antichrist. The tribulation. The rapture. Let's dive in.

CHAPTER 9

WHO IS THE ANTICHRIST—AND WHY DO SO MANY PEOPLE GET HIM WRONG?

Sorting Hype, History, and Hard Scripture

Let's talk about the key players of the end times, the cast of characters who even seasoned believers get a little wide-eyed about. I mean, you didn't pick up this book because you were hoping for another devotional about sheep and shepherds, right? No, this chapter is more *Avengers: Endgame*. You're here because you want to know who these people are. The ones the Bible warned us about. The ones who will take center stage when things go down for real. Think cosmic battle, global deception, and a villain whose entrance has been centuries in the making. Thanos may have snapped half the universe away, but our story's villain isn't fiction. The Antichrist is real, and his plan is already in motion.

If you dip your toe into researching the Antichrist online,

you'll find yourself falling headfirst into a rabbit hole deeper than your "just one more video" scroll on TikTok. Within hours, you'll be drowning in theories—some serious, and some straight-up wild. People have pointed fingers at everyone from the pope to US presidents to your favorite tech billionaire who probably owns half the internet. And yes, there are full-on camps, like end times Hogwarts houses, all with their own interpretation of who this mysterious figure really is.

But spoiler alert: We are not here to declare who the Antichrist is. That would be extremely unwise, unhelpful, and quite frankly, a little dangerous. People have made some confident guesses in history, and they were all wrong. Our goal here isn't to name names, point fingers, or claim some secret insight. It's to take an honest look at the theories that have circulated over time, explore what Scripture says (and doesn't say), and keep our eyes on Jesus in the process. Because trying to identify the Antichrist can quickly turn into a spiritual-distraction spiral. It's like doomscrolling while driving—you think you're paying attention, but you're actually veering off course and missing what really matters.

We're stepping back to understand the bigger picture, because before you can make sense of theories, you need to know where they're coming from (and no, not just from conspiracy theories or your cousin's Facebook timeline, although that does sound entertaining). Let's begin with the four main end times camps. There are four interpretive lenses: historicist, preterist, futurist, and idealist.[1] Each group approaches prophecy like it's solving a different kind of puzzle, with different pieces, timelines, and sometimes entirely different board games. Let's break them down one by one.

First, we've got the historicists. This crew sees prophecy as an unfolding timeline, one that stretches across centuries of church history and still speaks to us today. These guys are like, "Plot twist, the Antichrist already came, and it was the pope. Shocking, we know." This was the dominant view of Reformers like Martin Luther and John Calvin, who were convinced the beast of Revelation symbolized the papacy itself, not just one pope but the corrupt institution claiming divine authority. They weren't just winging it either; they claimed they had receipts, matching church corruption with apocalyptic symbols and scriptural imagery like horns and blasphemies.[2] One example is Luther's interpretation of the "man of sin . . . who . . . exalts himself above all that is called God" as the pope, who, he argued, sits in the temple of God and claims authority over God's Word, fitting Paul's warning in 2 Thessalonians 2:3–4.

The preterists, similar to the historicists, also believe that end times prophecies have already happened. Just that it was someone else. They come in cool and collected, saying, "Relax, guys, it already happened." They point to Emperor Nero (we'll get to him), who persecuted Christians and messed with the temple, giving escape-room energy with a side of Roman chaos. For them, Revelation wasn't written to predict a twenty-first-century microchip but to warn first-century believers about judgment that was literally around the corner. The beast? Probably Nero. The tribulation? The destruction of Jerusalem in AD 70. It's not that they don't believe in Jesus' return; they just think a lot of the fireworks already went off while we were still waiting for the show to start.

Then enter the futurists, those who interpret most of Revelation as describing future events. Think *Left Behind*, but with better CGI. They believe the Antichrist is a future global leader who'll rise during a seven-year tribulation. He will be charming, powerful, and super convincing . . . until he goes full villain mode. We're talking a spiritual Darth Vader, a political Joker, or a world-stage Voldemort. In this view, the church gets raptured (either before, during, or after the chaos), and the tribulation unfolds with dramatic judgments, global deception, and the eventual return of Christ to set things right. Futurists often interpret headlines like geopolitical tension in the Middle East, technology like microchips, or global government talk as signs we're inching closer to that prophetic countdown.

And then, the idealists roll up and say, "It's all a metaphor." They read prophecy symbolically or allegorically, focusing on timeless truths and the ongoing spiritual battle between good and evil rather than pinning events to specific dates or people. For them, the Antichrist isn't one dude in a suit; it's any system, spirit, or ideology that sets itself against Jesus. It's less "one man to watch for" and more like the *Stranger Things*' Upside Down, creeping through culture, shifting reality and hijacking minds. Basically, every time evil gains influence in the world, the beast is back on the move.

You also have the 1 John 4:3 crew. We haven't found their official fan-name yet, maybe something like Spirit of Antichrist Squad. The verse says, "Every spirit that does not confess Jesus is not from God. This is the spirit of the antichrist, which you heard was coming and now is in the world already" (ESV). Many read this and conclude that the Antichrist isn't some future end times villain but a spiritual force that's been lurking in the background since the first century. And while Scripture does talk about a spirit of antichrist, other passages also seem to describe a future individual—the man of lawlessness who will be revealed (2 Thessalonians 2:3–4), and the one who will make a covenant and halt the sacrifices (Daniel 9:27), so some believe it's not either-or but both-and. But not only does Scripture talk about the person; it talks about the process. And because of that process, we know that we haven't reached that point yet. There are still dominoes that have to fall. And they have to fall in order.

Now, before you spiral into an antichrist identity crisis (try saying that five times fast) trying to figure out who's who, here's the good news: The Bible gives us solid clues. God didn't leave us hanging with a cryptic emoji and a "figure it out" attitude. He laid out some seriously detailed descriptions of these end-time figures. Think of it as God handing us the script to the biggest blockbuster of all time, with Jesus as the ultimate Hero and the Antichrist as the villain who thinks he's clever, but we already know how the story ends. This story is biblically accurate and spiritually vital. If you're not yet impressed with our modern villain connections, hang in there as we unpack this figure.

The Dress Rehearsal Villains: A Trilogy

First, we have to do a little rewind to an ancient figure who's often seen as a major villain of the New Testament era: Nero. This guy ruled the Roman Empire around AD 54 and is infamous for his extreme cruelty toward Christians. We're talking burning-believers-with-garden-torches-level psychotic.[3] He was a narcissist to the max, with more ego than a rock star who just sold out Madison Square Garden . . . except his concerts were public executions. Crazy, right? Here's where it gets interesting.

In Revelation 13:18, we're given the famous "number of the beast": "This calls for wisdom: let the one who has understanding calculate the number of the beast, for it is the number of a man, and his number is 666" (ESV). Cue the *Indiana Jones* theme music, because God is basically inviting us to put on our decoding hats.

Now, Hebrew numerology, called *gematria*, assigns numerical values to letters. Back in Bible times, Hebrew (and even Greek and Latin) didn't use separate number symbols like we do today. Instead, every letter was also a number. If you wrote a name or word, it automatically had a numerical value. So Revelation 13:18 meant something specific to its readers. It wasn't just a spooky number for horror movies. You might be wondering, *What's the deal with 666?* Some scholars believe John was using gematria to point to a real person: Nero Caesar, the Roman emperor who brutally persecuted Christians. If you take the Greek spelling of his name, "Neron Kaisar," and transliterate it into Hebrew letters, then add up the value of each letter using gematria, guess what you get . . . 666.[4] Mic drop. Coincidence? Maybe. But in the language of prophecy, patterns matter.

Before we go all in on this, let's be clear. Nero is not the final Antichrist. He died by suicide at age thirty.[5] But in biblical literature, especially prophecy, there's this powerful theme called "types and shadows." Like how Abraham offering up Isaac in Genesis is a type and shadow of God offering His Son, Jesus. It's a spiritual echo. Scripture is full of them. Nero is one of those echoes, a shadow of the Antichrist who is still to come.

According to 2 Thessalonians 2:3–4, there will be a man, the ultimate Antichrist, who will exalt himself above everything called God and even sit in God's temple, proclaiming himself to be God. Not subtle at all. This guy isn't spiritually confused; he's on a full-blown mission to deceive the world and wipe out the saints. So if you're imagining someone slick, persuasive, media-savvy, and weirdly charming while being spiritually toxic, you're not far off.

The profile of the Antichrist of the last days isn't one that's random. We don't have to guess what he'll be like. The books of Daniel and Revelation give us vivid imagery and plain statements about him. This guy will rise to global power; he'll be celebrated, praised, feared, and eventually worshiped by many. It'll be so deceptive that even the elect would be fooled if they're not rooted in the Word (Matthew 24:24).

Revelation 13:7 tells us "It was granted to him to make war with the saints and to overcome them." This guy isn't just bad news for the world; he's coming directly for God's people.

Now if you go back even further, you meet Antiochus IV Epiphanes.[6] He's the prequel villain to Nero's full-blown franchise. He ruled in the second century BC and made Jewish life feel like a horror movie. He outlawed circumcision, burned Torah scrolls, and desecrated the temple by sacrificing pigs on the altar. He called himself "Epiphanes," meaning "God manifest." Like Nero, Antiochus was a major type and shadow of the Antichrist to come.

So now we've got layers: Antiochus as the historical example, Nero as another shadow, and the Antichrist as the ultimate fulfillment. This is how prophecy works: It echoes through time until it climaxes in one final event.

Now enter Nimrod—yes, the same guy whose name now gets used as an insult in cartoons, but in biblical terms, he was a big deal. Genesis 10:8–10 tells us that Nimrod was a mighty warrior and the first king of Babylon. He's associated with building the Tower of Babel in Genesis 11, where humanity tried to unify under one language and one government, without God. In prophetic tradition, Nimrod is seen as the prototype of a God-defying world ruler. You know, the kind of guy who tries to "bring the world together" but is actually trying to edge out the Creator in the process.

Each of these characters—Nero, Antiochus, and Nimrod—are spiritual blueprints. They give us context for the Antichrist. Think of them as the teaser trailers. Now, it's our job to pay attention to the full-length feature film coming soon . . . that may be already playing.

CHAPTER 10

HOW COULD WE FALL FOR THE GREATEST CON JOB EVER?

A Checklist for the Coming Deception

Why did God give us so many clues, so many shadows, and so many prophecies about this one figure? It's like He wants us to recognize him. God doesn't waste words. Every passage is there for a reason. Like Amos 3:7 says, "Surely the Sovereign LORD does nothing without revealing his plan to his servants the prophets" (NIV).

So we decided to make a checklist. A full-on biblical profile of this guy so that when he does rise to power, if he hasn't started to already, you'll have more than conspiracy theories from social media videos to go on. Looking at the books of Daniel and Revelation, where the Antichrist's full profile seems to be revealed, we can gain some key profile characteristics for him.

Because the truth is, Scripture didn't just tell us that he's coming. It told us what he'll look like. It told us what he'll say. How he'll act. And how to make sure we're not caught off guard when headlines start to mirror prophecy. Let's get into it.

The Antichrist Checklist

Now that we've met the shadows—Nero, Antiochus, and Nimrod—it's time to talk about the real deal: the Antichrist. The man who steps onto the global stage with charisma, power, and a whole lot of demonic backing. But contrary to popular belief, he won't come wearing a "Hi, I'm the Antichrist" name tag. No horns. No cape. No creepy horror movie soundtrack. In fact, he's going to look like everything the world wants: a unifier, a peace broker, a problem solver. People will call him brilliant. Compassionate. Revolutionary. And that's the most dangerous part.

The Bible doesn't want you guessing in the dark. It gives us signs. Descriptions. Clues. If you're paying attention, you won't be shocked; you'll be ready. So let's break down the Antichrist's profile. Think of this as your spiritual intelligence briefing. You're not just a reader, you're a watcher. Let's go.

He Rises from the Ashes of the Empire (Daniel 7:7–8; Revelation 13:1)

Daniel saw a terrifying beast with ten horns, representing ten kings or kingdoms. Then, "another horn, a little one" (Daniel 7:8) rises and uproots three of the original ten. Revelation 13 echoes this image with a beast rising from the sea (symbol of the nations), having ten horns and seven heads, combining elements of previous empires (lion, bear, leopard). We know that sounds kind of crazy! But we'll make sense of this together.

This is the Antichrist's origin story. He doesn't start out with total power. He emerges from what seems to be political reshuffling, possibly a confederation of nations, possibly a global crisis that leads to realignment.

Clue: He will come from within an alliance or empire and rise quickly by removing rivals. (Watch for major political turnover.)

He's a Charismatic Problem Solver (Daniel 8:23–25)

He's described as "a fierce-looking king, a master of intrigue" (Daniel 8:23 NIV). He'll be intelligent, persuasive, and able to "cause deceit to prosper" (v. 25). Think: the kind of leader who talks his way into peace treaties while setting the stage for domination behind the scenes.

Clue: He uses charm, not brute force, at first. The world falls in love before it falls under control.

He Makes a False Peace (Daniel 9:27)

"He will confirm a covenant with many for one 'seven'" (Daniel 9:27 NIV). This "seven" refers to a seven-year period, and this treaty is seen as a key marker of the Antichrist's rise. It could be a political agreement, likely involving Israel and the Middle East. The world will celebrate him as the man who finally brought peace. But halfway through, he breaks it.

Clue: He's a dealmaker. Watch for someone who brokers peace in impossible places, especially in Jerusalem.

He Sets Himself Up as God (2 Thessalonians 2:3–4)

Paul was blunt: The man of sin will "exalt himself over everything that is called God" and sit in the temple of God, "proclaiming himself to be God" (2 Thessalonians 2:4 NIV). This is the blasphemy of all blasphemies. It's not metaphorical. It's literal. There will be a rebuilt temple, and this guy will walk in like he owns the place.

Clue: He doesn't just oppose God. He replaces God. This is where things get openly demonic.

He Performs Signs and Wonders (Revelation 13:13–14)

"He performs great signs, so that he even makes fire come down from heaven on the earth in the sight of men. And he deceives those who dwell on the earth by those signs which he was granted to do in the sight of the beast" (Revelation 13:13–14). This isn't just politics; it's supernatural deception. This is where the False Prophet (his hype man essentially) enters the chat, pushing the world to worship him.

Clue: He'll bring fire from heaven. Miracles. False signs. People will be so amazed, they'll think he's divine. But miracles alone don't prove truth. Evil figures in Scripture also performed miraculous or supernatural acts. Pharaoh's magicians mimicked Moses' signs (Exodus 7:10–12) and the sorcerer Simon amazed crowds in Samaria with his magic (Acts 8:9–11). Supernatural power doesn't always equal divine truth. If it doesn't align with Scripture, it's a setup. Sensitivity and discernment from the Holy Spirit will be vital.

He Persecutes the Saints (Revelation 13:7)

This is one of the hardest truths to swallow. The Antichrist will seemingly be allowed to wage war against God's people, and it'll appear that he's winning, temporarily anyway (Revelation 13:7). Many believers will likely be martyred. This isn't the sanitized, Sunday-school version of faith. This is real spiritual and even physical warfare. The type of warfare that some in different parts of the world are experiencing even as you read this. This isn't the "persecution" that's experienced in the comment sections and digital spaces that are social media and beyond. This is the real deal.

Clue: Persecution will ramp up under his rule, especially against Bible-believing Christians. Start asking questions and stay alert.

He Controls Commerce: The Mark of the Beast (Revelation 13:16–17)

Here it is: the infamous mark of the beast. No one can buy or sell without it. This is about control. Economic control becomes spiritual loyalty. The mark isn't just about convenience; it's about allegiance.

There's been many different claims and assumptions about the mark of the beast. Whether it's a chip, a digital ID, or something we haven't seen yet, Scripture gives us a few clear indications of what the mark will entail. Revelation 13:16 says it will be "a mark on their right hand or on their foreheads." We've discussed and entertained different things as to how this will be administered. We've even talked about it at length in a couple of podcast episodes.[1] If you would have mentioned artificial intelligence playing a part in the mark of the beast and the Antichrist even five years ago, the majority of people would have laughed at and dismissed you. Now? It doesn't seem too far-fetched. But that's a conversation for another time. (Feel free to dig deeper on that one on your own. It gets crazy.)

Clue: Watch for global systems that tie commerce to surrender of freedoms. If you have to compromise faith to participate, you're looking at a prototype.

He Has a Deadly Wound, and He Heals (Revelation 13:3)

In one of the most bizarre twists in Revelation, the Antichrist appears to die, possibly an assassination attempt or some kind of "deadly wound" (13:3). But then, he miraculously recovers, and the world is in awe. Scripture says that this wound would be fatal. So this won't just be a recovery from a regular gunshot or a stabbing or something. It's going to be something that should have killed him. Appearing to beat death—sound familiar?

Clue: A fake resurrection = a counterfeit Christ. It's designed to imitate Jesus and deceive the masses.

He's Backed by the Dragon (Revelation 13:2, 4)

The source of the Antichrist's power? Satan himself. He doesn't rise on charisma alone; he's demonically empowered. Revelation says, "The dragon gave [the beast] his power, his throne, and great authority" (13:2). He is a literal agent of hell. The idea of Satan as a dragon isn't a new thing. Happy hunting on that one as well! It gets wild.

Clue: Behind every smile, speech, and policy of the Antichrist is a dark spirit. Discernment is not optional; it's your lifeline.

He May Have Tribal Ties to Dan (Revelation 7, 14)

Here's where things gets a little more *Stranger Things*-esque. There's a theory that the Antichrist might actually be connected to the tribe of Dan, one of the original twelve tribes of Israel.[2] Now, jump to Revelation chapters 7 and 14, where we get introduced to this mysterious group called the 144,000. Basically, there are 12,000 people from each of the twelve tribes who are sealed and protected by God during the chaos of the end times. Think of them as God's elite spiritual task force, like the Navy SEALs of truth telling in the last days. Many believe that they'll be spreading the gospel and initiating revival during the end times.

But here's the interesting part. When you look at the list of tribes that make up this select 144,000, Dan is left out. Like . . . no invite to the group chat. That'd be like talking about Michael Jordan's championships and leaving out Scottie Pippen. It just wouldn't make sense. Unless it does. Some folks think that's a clue; the tribe's exclusion might hint at something deeper, maybe even a connection to betrayal or evil. Kinda gives off major Slytherin energy, if you know what we mean. It's not a smoking gun, but it's one of those biblical breadcrumbs that makes you go, "Wait . . . what's really going on here?"

Let's briefly go back to the ancient origin story of the twelve tribes for some context. In Genesis 49, Jacob gives each of his sons a prophecy about their tribe's future. When he gets to Dan, he drops this: "Dan shall be a serpent by the way, a viper by the path, that bites the horse's heels so that its rider shall fall backward" (v. 17). Talk about a crazy prophecy to be spoken. Imagine you and your brothers being called out by your father, who says, "Gather around so I can tell you what will happen to you in days to come" (v. 1 NIV). You listen as your brothers get these awesome words and then you get that. Talk about a wild turn of events!

A serpent? Why that animal? From Genesis 3 onward, serpents in Scripture consistently represent deception and evil. The serpent deceived Eve in the garden (Genesis 3:1–5), and

Revelation identifies Satan himself as "that ancient serpent" (Revelation 12:9, 20:2 NIV). There's not a single positive portrayal of a serpent in Scripture; they always signal danger, deception, or satanic association. And to make it even more interesting, early church fathers (like Irenaeus and Hippolytus) believed this was a direct clue to the tribe of Dan's dark future, possibly even that the Antichrist himself would come from Dan. Hippolytus said, "Dan is not reckoned in the Apocalypse among the saved tribes. Hence the Antichrist is to spring from that tribe."[3]

So if someone were to claim the Antichrist comes from the tribe of Dan, how could we verify it? DNA testing sounds like a modern go-to, but it's not that simple. The twelve tribes of Israel dispersed thousands of years ago, and much of the detailed lineage has been lost or mixed into other people groups. Today, there isn't a reliable genetic marker that can say with certainty, "This person is from the tribe of Dan." But beyond DNA, there are other things to consider. Prophecy watchers often look at geographical clues, like whether a person's ancestry traces back to regions historically linked to Dan, such as parts of northern Israel or coastal areas near the Mediterranean. Some even look at symbolism in names, behaviors, or affiliations that echo characteristics attributed to Dan in Scripture, like deception. Then there's spiritual discernment: Many believe the Antichrist will carry a powerful and deceptive charisma that spiritually aligns with the rebellious nature associated with Dan.

While we may never get hard, scientific proof, a combination of historical patterns, biblical hints, and spiritual clues could give insight into that connection. In the end, it's less about lab results and more about understanding the prophetic and spiritual patterns that Scripture lays out. But the moment someone stands up and claims to be God in a temple, you better believe we're demanding a 23andMe and Ancestry.com test pronto!

It's a theory. Not gospel. But it is pretty crazy how much sense it could make in the overall plot.

Enter the Nephilim: Giants, Hybrid Bloodlines, and Preflood Chaos

If Dan is the serpent tribe, the Nephilim are the shadow race, the hybrid offspring of fallen angels and human women. Yes, that's in the Bible: "The Nephilim were on the earth in those days—and also afterward—when the sons of God went to the daughters of humans and had children by them. They were the heroes of old, men of renown" (Genesis 6:4 NIV). Now we won't do a full-on deep dive about the Nephilim and the history of fallen angels and rebellious figures in this book, but here's a bird's-eye view. If you want to really dig into it, we've got multiple podcast episodes about it![4]

Nephilim caused the original supernatural freakout before the flood. Think: ancient giants, corrupted DNA, and enough violence and wickedness to make God hit the reset button via Noah's ark. The word *Nephilim* comes from the root *naphal*, meaning "to fall."[5] These weren't just big dudes; they were part of a dark rebellion that sought to contaminate humanity's line.

Here's where it gets suspiciously connected. A theory that has been popularized in certain end times prophecy circles suggest that the spirit of the Nephilim, or even remnants of their corrupted DNA, could carry forward through certain bloodlines, possibly even making their way into the Antichrist's origins.[6]

Sound wild? Sure. It's a fringe theory at best. But when you study the prophetic layers of Scripture, especially passages connecting serpents, giants, and demonic influence, it feels worth at least acknowledging these ideas exist, even if we hold them loosely.

So here is the potential crossover theory. Go there with us for a moment: Dan + Nephilim = Future Antichrist? This is where our investigative board with red strings comes out:

- Dan is prophesied as a serpent = deceiver.
- Dan is excluded from Revelation's "sealed tribes" = judgment or corruption.
- The OG Dan himself settled in the northernmost part of Israel, where idolatry and pagan practices were common.
- The fallen angels in Genesis 6 created a race of giants = the Nephilim.
- After the flood, Nephilim-like figures show up again (Numbers 13:33).
- Some believe these bloodlines continued, contaminating tribes like Dan.
- Therefore, the Antichrist may rise from a corrupted lineage, both physically and spiritually, combining serpent deception and Nephilim defiance.

Could the final world leader be a composite villain, a spiritual descendant of the serpent, the Nephilim, and the most rebellious bloodline in Israel's history? Maybe.

While we don't have to get too obsessed with DNA tests for the Antichrist just yet, here's what this all tells us. First, God leaves prophetic fingerprints on history. The omission of Dan and the pattern of rebellion are there for a reason. Second, Satan has been playing the long game. From Eden to Babel to Babylon to Rome, and perhaps even Dan and the Nephilim, he's been trying to hijack God's plan since day one. Third, types and shadows matter. God gives us previews. Nero, Antiochus, Nimrod, Dan, and the Nephilim are like cinematic foreshadowing for the ultimate Antichrist. And last, you were never meant to be caught off guard. The Bible gives us intel so we can discern the times, recognize deception, and stay anchored in truth—something we'll continue to echo in this book.

Stay Close to the Real; Spot the Fake

Paul wrote in 2 Thessalonians that the man of lawlessness won't be revealed until a certain point (2:3 NIV). Jesus Himself said many false prophets and false messiahs would come, and to stay alert (Matthew 24:11, 24). So while it's intriguing to connect the dots (and admittedly kind of fun in a mystery-thriller kind of way), the real point of all the Antichrist talk isn't to freak out or point fingers; it's to stay close to the real Christ. It's to know the original so well that the fake becomes obvious.

The real point of all the Antichrist talk isn't to freak out or point fingers; it's to stay close to the real Christ. It's to know the original so well that the fake becomes obvious.

What if the greatest danger isn't that the Antichrist shows up wearing red horns and announcing world domination? What if the danger is that he looks really good, compassionate, visionary, and peaceful? What if he doesn't come with a pitchfork but a platform?

And what if the only way to avoid deception is intimacy with Jesus?

This chapter, like the others, isn't meant to scare you. We hope more than anything it's an invitation to sharpen your discernment. Because if there's one thing we've learned from this wild investigation, it's that theories will come and go. The headlines will keep changing. The symbols might get misread and misinterpreted. But the truth? That's eternal.

Let's end this chapter with hope. The Antichrist's rise may look inevitable. But so is his fall. The Antichrist is doomed to fail (Revelation 19:19–21). Because no matter how terrifying this guy sounds, his end is written in stone. Jesus Himself returns. No negotiation. No rematch. Just the Word of God riding a white horse, and the Antichrist is thrown into the lake of fire.

So why the checklist? Because God didn't want us asleep at the wheel. He didn't give us these prophetic signs so that we could argue timelines and headlines. He gave us the profile of this figure so we could be watchful, rooted, and ready. The Antichrist may look like progress. He may sound like hope. He may act like peace. But if he checks these boxes, he's not a savior; he's a counterfeit. If the world is preparing for his rise, then we have to be preparing for Christ's return.

CHAPTER 11

WE DON'T KNOW THE DAY, BUT WE CAN READ THE ROOM

When "No One Knows the Hour" Isn't the End of the Conversation

Have you ever found yourself staring up at the sky wondering, *Could today be the day?* Maybe you've been at home and heard a distant train blowing its horn, and if you were honest, you thought for just one second, *Oh no, this is it!* Don't worry, you're definitely not alone. We're sure several of us have woken up in an empty home wondering if we got left behind. The question of Jesus' return has sparked curiosity, debate, and even confusion throughout the centuries. But what exactly does Scripture say about knowing the timing of this monumental event?

Hopefully by now you're beginning to see the road map that we believe the Word of God has laid out for us. Breadcrumbs sprinkled throughout the text that have been there all along. As we've been trying to piece all of them together, we believe that there may be even more than what's already been investigated throughout this book thus far. But we want to keep digging a little deeper. The heart of this section addresses questions that believers of all backgrounds and upbringings have pondered throughout generations: When will the "rapture" and "tribulation period" actually be? Are we able to identify scriptures that give us a better insight to these questions? Does Scripture provide clear insight on this question?

As we mentioned earlier, there is a verse that people often use when talking about the last days, specifically the rapture. Jesus plainly stated in Matthew 24:36, "Of that day and hour no one knows, not even the angels of heaven, but my Father only." The Greek words used here, *hemera* ("day") and *hora* ("hour"),[1] underline a precise moment unknown to all except God the Father Himself. Again, the idea that this one verse can put a screeching halt to all eschatology conversations is incomplete. God is all about revealing things to His body for the sake of preparation and understanding.

Ignorance of a topic doesn't have to equate to avoidance. This is some heavy stuff, we get it! The last thing you want is to start stamping exact dates all over and be misleading. But how awesome of God, who didn't give us a spirit of fear, to desire that we know how things might play out. So while we will not know the exact day or hour, Scripture suggests that we should recognize the season of His return. So much so that in Matthew 16, Jesus rebuked the religious leaders for failing to discern prophetic seasons: "When it is evening you say, 'It will be fair weather, for the sky is red'; and in the morning, 'It will be foul weather today, for the sky is red and threatening.' Hypocrites! You know how to discern the face of the sky, but you cannot discern the signs of the times" (vv. 2–3).

Could this rebuke imply that spiritual discernment of prophetic seasons isn't just encouraged, but it's expected? If Jesus rebuked the Pharisees for not recognizing the signs of His first coming, how much more vital is it for the church today to recognize the signs of His second coming? A lot of believers are okay with living in the unknown and clinging to ignorance. When this happens, it becomes so easy to dismiss the urgency of discerning prophetic signs. Could the Pharisees' failure stand as a cautionary tale for today's believers? Based on Scripture, spiritual discernment doesn't seem optional; rather, it's critical.

In 1 Thessalonians 5:1–6, the apostle Paul exhorts believers to remain spiritually alert and discerning as the return of the Lord draws near. He wrote,

> But concerning the times and the seasons, brethren, you have no need that I should write to you. For you yourselves know perfectly that the day of the Lord so comes as a thief in the night. For when they say, "Peace and safety!" then sudden destruction comes upon them, as labor pains upon a pregnant woman. And they shall not escape. But you, brethren, are not in darkness, so that this Day should overtake you as a thief. You are all sons of light and sons of the day. We are not of the night nor of darkness. Therefore let us not sleep, as others do, but let us watch and be sober.

In verse 1 Paul made a distinct point using two Greek words for "times" and "seasons": *chronos* and *kairos.*[2] *Chronos* refers to linear, chronological time, days, months, and years as they pass.

Kairos, however, denotes specific, divinely appointed moments, seasons when God moves according to His purposes. In using both terms, Paul communicated that believers should already be aware of God's overarching timeline as well as sensitive to the prophetic seasons unfolding before them.

Paul was essentially expressing that you don't need another fresh prophetic word or new teaching about God's timing; you've already been equipped. You've been taught to watch, to stay ready, and to live alert. His warning is not about knowing the date of Christ's return, but about cultivating spiritual awareness so that the day does not overtake us unexpectedly, like a thief in the night.

Because of this distinction, the awareness spoken about in the text is not given to everyone. The implication is clear: Spiritual passivity and slumber are marks of those outside of the light. But for those in Christ, vigilance and sobriety are not suggestions; they are a way of life. Can you imagine if a close friend of yours knew when something completely life-altering was going to take place and didn't share it with you but rather left you in the dark? They would not be considered a very good friend. And even more so, imagine if that was your father. How gracious our Father is to invite us into spiritual insights through His Word that give us a fresh fire for the people of God and the Great Commission!

Paul echoed this same urgency in Romans 13:11–12: "And do this, knowing the time [*kairos*], that now it is high time to awake out of sleep: for now is our salvation is nearer than when we first believed. The night is far spent, the day is at hand. Therefore let us cast off the works of darkness, and let us put on the armor of light."

Here again, *kairos* indicates a set, divine moment, an

opportune season requiring action. Paul called believers to wake up, not just physically but spiritually. The nearness of Christ's return demands that we throw off compromise, cast off the works of darkness, and clothe ourselves with light. It is not enough to know the signs; we must live in response to them. As we continue to see different headlines, shocking global stories, and countless pieces of content flooding conversations as well as digital spaces, every conversation should end with hope in Jesus. Our response should be urgency to deepen and/or establish a relationship with Jesus, led by His Spirit.

We know that this expectation for discernment and readiness is not a New Testament idea alone. The prophet Daniel was told that the full understanding of his end-time vision would not be available immediately. Instead, it would be unsealed and understood only at the appointed *kairos*, the "time of the end."

Daniel 12:8–10 recorded this moment: "I heard, but I did not understand. So I asked, 'My lord, what will the outcome of all this be?' He replied, 'Go your way, Daniel, because the words are rolled up and sealed until the time of the end. Many will be purified, made spotless and refined, but the wicked will continue to be wicked. None of the wicked will understand, but those who are wise will understand'" (NIV).

Here we see a final truth. Understanding is not promised to everyone. Those who live in rebellion will remain blind to the signs of the times. But the "wise will understand." In other words, those who walk in reverence, righteousness, and relationship with God will have eyes to see and ears to hear what the Spirit is saying in the last days.

In Matthew 24:32–33, Jesus expanded this concept using a vivid analogy: "Now learn this parable from the fig tree: When its branch has already become tender and puts forth leaves, you know that summer is near. So you also, when you see all these things, know that it is near—at the doors!" Here, Christ clearly emphasized that certain signs will signal the nearing season of His return. Just as the tender branches of the fig tree indicate summer, so prophetic signs will point unmistakably toward His imminent return.

Among these signs, earlier in that very chapter of Matthew, we encounter powerful imagery. Verse 7 says, "For nation will rise against nation, and kingdom against kingdom. And there will be famines, pestilences, and earthquakes in various places." Interestingly, the original Greek text translates "nation" as *ethnos*, implying not only governmental conflicts but deep ethnic conflict and tension among different people groups. We're witnessing exactly this in our time, all over the world—escalating ethnic conflicts that could certainly reveal an undeniable alignment with Christ's prophetic words.

Another crucial sign is the nation of Israel itself. In 1948, Israel became a nation again, fulfilling ancient prophecy. Could this have been a crucial marking of the beginning of the prophetic "fig tree" season? Scripture points explicitly to Israel as God's prophetic time clock. The majority of the events on this "road map" are connected to Israel. As believers, understanding Israel's role becomes vital, especially regarding events like the rebuilding of the Third Temple and the necessary red heifer sacrifices. So not if, but *when*, these dominoes start to fall, we can confidently know we are entering into a new season of biblical proportions.

Yet sadly, so many people today remain oblivious to these critical prophetic signs. And don't get us wrong, we recognize the overwhelming importance of the Great Commission, loving like Christ, and caring for our neighbors. This discussion certainly isn't to diminish or devalue those mandates at all. But to not acknowledge and engage this discussion contradicts the clear expectation that God's people would understand prophetic seasons.

The Bible emphasizes this through the sons of Issachar, "who had understanding of the times, to know what Israel ought to do" (1 Chronicles 12:32). In our time, believers who discern prophetic seasons will lead and instruct many, turning countless souls toward righteousness and to be awakened to what God is doing around the world in the last days. As we continue to see wild headlines and news stories flooding our screens and social media, there will be a global shift. We'll start to see countless people trying to interpret what God has already explained through the text. None of the conclusions drawn will be new concepts or ideas. It's all found in the Word of God. Our prayer is that this book would help you have an "understanding of the times." The last days don't have to be filled with confusion.

But what exactly are "the last days" or the tribulation season? In Acts 2 Peter quoted Joel's prophecy, saying, "And it shall come to pass in the last days, says God, that I will pour out of My Spirit on all flesh" (v. 17). Peter clearly identified Pentecost as the initiation of the last days. But if this was two thousand years ago, how could we still be in the last days? If you're a numbers person like we are, this thought process will be really cool to unpack. And if you're not, just hang with us; this is still pretty awesome! And we promise it will be way simpler than the Daniel numbers breakdown earlier.

Math Avengers, Assemble One More Time

The key to how we could still be in the last days lies in understanding and unpacking God's potential timeline. Time works differently in heaven. So nerd out with us for just a moment! There is a scripture where Peter is speaking of "the day of the Lord" (2 Peter 3:10). A couple of verses earlier he'd explained, "With the Lord one day is as a thousand years, and a thousand years as one day" (v. 8). Scripture frequently illustrates this pattern. Hosea 6:2 seems to prophetically declare that "after two days He will revive us; on the third day He will raise us up." If we interpret a day as a thousand years, then two thousand years from Christ's first coming brings us precisely into the threshold of the third prophetic "day." Now, wouldn't that be crazy? But wait, there's more! Cue the infomercial voice.

If we expand on the idea Peter introduced, there may be things that we've missed. Consider the pattern: roughly four thousand years from Adam to Jesus, two thousand years from Jesus to our present time, marking a total of six thousand years, or six prophetic "days." The number six is associated with humanity throughout Scripture. Man was created on the sixth day (Genesis 1:26–31), and even in Revelation 13:18, the mark of the beast is 666, described as "the number of a man." Scripture points clearly to the seventh day as God's day, a day of rest, restoration, and the rule of Christ. If we are at the conclusion of humanity's sixth prophetic day, the dawn of God's Sabbath rest, the seventh day, must be near. What?! Some of you may have read that and remained calm. But if this is truly the connection Scripture is making for us, all the breadcrumbs are turning into something incredible. But there are still more numbers in Scripture that we have to investigate and connect the dots on.

Scripture seems to further confirm this prophetic time frame through Jubilee cycles. Now, Jubilee is different from the Shemitah cycle we discussed earlier. The Shemitah cycle happens every seven years, Jubilee occurs every fifty years (after seven cycles of seven years). Leviticus 25 outlines Jubilee as occurring every fifty years, marked by the blowing of a trumpet. During this year there would be a forgiveness of debts, reconciliation on another level to God and to others, a returning of land that was misappropriated, all sorts of things. The Hebrew word *Yobel*, translated "Jubilee," literally means trumpet. Remarkably, the apostle Paul identified Christ's return with the trumpet sound (1 Thessalonians 4:16). Just as the trumpet signaled liberty and restoration in Israel, so, too, will a trumpet announce the ultimate restoration at Christ's return.

Let's keep digging! Genesis 6:3 states, "My Spirit shall not strive with man forever . . . his days shall be one hundred and twenty years."

Even when it comes to this number, the math could be revealing a deeper prophetic significance. One hundred twenty Jubilee cycles, each fifty years, equal exactly six thousand years. So what could this six-thousand-year time frame actually represent? It seems to mirror the six days of creation, which could be prophetically foreshadowing six "days" (six thousand years) of human history before entering God's seventh day of rest, the millennial reign of Christ, which is the one-thousand-year period after Jesus returns where He rules the earth in perfect peace, justice, and power, with believers reigning alongside Him (Revelation 20). Just as God created the world in six days and rested on the seventh, prophetic history may follow the same pattern: six thousand years of human striving followed by one thousand years of divine rest and restoration (Revelation 20:4–6).

According to many biblical chronologies, including those based on the Masoretic text, creation is estimated around 4000 BC. If that's even close to accurate, then we're living somewhere around the year 6000 on God's prophetic calendar. That means we're not just approaching the end; we could be in it!

Now that might be crazy to just us, but it is amazing to think that all of this may not be just a coincidence. Could it be that once again, the Bible's numeric symbolism perfectly aligns, reinforcing that we could be nearing the end of this prophetic period?

Scripture repeats this numeric pattern: Moses lived exactly 120 years (Deuteronomy 34:7), and then the season of entering the promised land commenced. At Pentecost, 120 disciples received the Holy Spirit and we saw the birth of the church in a mighty way (Acts 1:15). Maybe these recurring patterns aren't coincidental. Maybe they're divine signposts pointing unmistakably toward the culmination of human history. Maybe you think we are thinking way too much into this. Or maybe God has been giving us the signs all along!

CHAPTER 12

NOW LET'S TALK ABOUT THE RAPTURE

What If It's Not the Church's Escape Plan?

We've walked through history, crunched the numbers, and traced the patterns. And that leads us to the unavoidable question. The one that's sparked debates, split churches, and filled comment sections for decades: What happens to the Church when things get intense? Are we taken out before the storm, or called to stand strong in the middle of it? The answer matters more than you might think. Because if we're truly living in the season we believe we are, then how we prepare, whether for escape or endurance, could be the difference between standing firm and being caught off guard.

So let's talk about the rapture. *Dun dun dun!* This refers to when Christ will gather believers. First Thessalonians 4 clearly describes the event: Christ descending, a trumpet sounding, and believers meeting Him in the air. Yet controversy arises over the timing. Will the rapture occur before, during, or after the tribulation? For years there have been arguments for all three.

Before we dive into this further, let's reset the scene once more. We're at a coffee shop, remember? Latte in hand (or your favorite tea for all our non-coffee drinkers), having discussions on things that are secondary to salvation. Many of you will have varying opinions about when this prophetic event takes place. We aren't strangers to disagreement. We receive hundreds of comments and messages all the time. We can still hang, high-five, and share a pastry from our favorite coffee shop together. We encourage you to do some research and come to your own conclusion. Here's where we've landed after doing our own deep dive to investigate this.

First things first. Let's address something that you may or may not be aware of. The word *rapture* doesn't appear anywhere in the Bible. Not once. So where did this term come from, and what does Scripture actually say? The word most commonly translated as "rapture" comes from the Greek word *harpazo*, which appears in 1 Thessalonians 4:17: "Then we who are alive and remain shall be caught up together with them in the clouds to meet the Lord in the air." The phrase "caught up" is *harpazo*, meaning to seize, snatch away, or catch up suddenly.[1]

A fourth-century Christian scholar named Jerome was tasked by Pope Damasus to translate the Bible from Greek and Hebrew into Latin, creating what became known as the Vulgate.[2] In his translation he rendered *harpazo* as *rapio*, from which we get our English word *rapture*. So while the concept of being "caught up" is absolutely biblical, the specific term *rapture* is actually a translation choice that stuck around for centuries. We'll use that term so you don't have to keep saying the word *harpazo*.

Paul addressed the rapture directly: "That Day [the coming of Christ] will not come unless the falling away comes first, and the man of sin is revealed . . . [who] sits as God in the temple" (2 Thessalonians 2:3–4). It seems that the rapture, this "gathering together," does not occur until after the Antichrist's appearance and desecration of the Third Temple.

Jesus seemed to reinforce this timeline, stating, "Immediately after the tribulation . . . they will see the Son of Man coming. . . . He will send His angels . . . and they will gather together His elect" (Matthew 24:29–31). Notice the consistency of Scripture: the gathering of believers, the sound of a trumpet, the visible return of Christ—all seem to occur distinctly after the tribulation. It seems as if these key end times scriptures point to this moment happening after this tribulation period takes place.

If that's the case, it's crucial that believers recognize this timing to avoid deception. Those expecting a pre-tribulation rapture might become vulnerable during the tribulation, caught unprepared. And we will talk some about this. But before we do so, we have to first talk about how the idea of a "pre-trib rapture" entered the mainstream church conversation.

Pre-Tribulation Rapture

If you grew up in church, you might have heard things like, "We're not going to be here for the tribulation," or maybe you saw those *Left Behind* movies that had Kirk Cameron dodging earthquakes while the Antichrist was giving press conferences. For some of us, the pre-tribulation rapture idea is so familiar, we assume it's always been taught. But the truth is, this view is only about two hundred years old, and a big part of why it went viral in the Christian world is thanks partly to a man named Cyrus Ingerson Scofield.

Cyrus I. Scofield was a Confederate-soldier-turned-lawyer-turned-preacher. After coming to faith, he became a pastor and Bible teacher. But what really put his name in the history books (and in the backs of a million pews) was his Scofield Reference Bible, first published in 1909 and later expanded in 1917. Now, this wasn't just any Bible. It was a Bible with commentary notes printed directly next to the scriptures, giving readers a kind of built-in theological road map. Sounds helpful, right? It was. But it also created something subtle and powerful: the idea that Scofield's interpretations carried as much weight as the verses themselves. And one of those interpretations was the pre-tribulation rapture.[3] Let's break it down.

The pre-tribulation rapture suggests that Jesus will return suddenly to take the church out of the world *before* a seven-year tribulation period begins. It's like the escape hatch before all the chaos unfolds—wars, plagues, Antichrist drama, and everything Revelation-level intense. Supporters point to verses like:

- 1 Thessalonians 4:16–17: "Caught up together with them in the clouds"
- 1 Corinthians 15:51–52: "In the twinkling of an eye"
- Revelation 3:10: "I also will keep you from the hour of trial"

Now, the pre-trib view sees this as a separate event from the second coming, where Jesus comes back visibly, in power, to judge the world and reign. Contrary to what some might think, Scofield didn't invent this view. The credit (or controversy) goes back to a man named John Nelson Darby, a British preacher in the 1830s and a key figure in the Plymouth Brethren movement. Scofield took Darby's theology and made it accessible.[4] He baked it into his study Bible, and that Bible spread like wildfire. It was printed, reprinted, taught in Bible colleges, and used by generations of preachers across America. Want to know why most prophecy conferences in the twentieth century taught the rapture as a given? Scofield. The Scofield Reference Bible didn't just teach; it shaped. It became a lens through which Christians read the Bible. His footnotes trained people to interpret Scripture through a literal, futuristic, pretribulational lens, especially when it came to end times and Israel. Churches, seminaries, and Christian publishers latched onto the pre-trib view and ran with it, fueling everything from *Left Behind* to Sunday-school charts with timelines and trumpet sounds.

But the pre-trib view isn't clearly spelled out in Scripture the way some think. It's a system of interpretation, built by connecting verses from different books and reading them through a specific lens. Some scholars argue the rapture is pre-trib; others say mid-trib, post-trib, or no rapture at all but one visible return of Jesus. In other words, it's all theory, not dogma.

A Historical View of the "Coming of the Lord"

So how does it all happen? How can we better understand this event that's been a two-thousand-year waiting room? During all of this research, we discovered something interesting. There's an important word used in the Bible when referencing end-time events that you may have never heard explained before. The word is *parousia*. This Greek word shows up all over the New Testament whenever the authors talk about Jesus coming back, or the "coming of the Lord." But here's the thing—first-century believers knew exactly what this meant, and we may have completely lost the plot.

Parousia wasn't just a generic word for "arrival." It was actually describing a very specific cultural event that everyone back then would have been familiar with. Picture this: When a king, emperor, or foreign dignitary was coming to visit your city, there was a whole process called a *parousia*.[5] Here's how it worked. First, the city would send out a delegation, or a greeting party, to meet the approaching king while he was still on his way. They would travel out, sometimes for miles, to meet him and honor his arrival. Then, this same group would escort the king back to their city, accompanying him for his grand entrance. Are you seeing where this is going?

This wasn't unusual or confusing to first-century readers. When Paul wrote about the *parousia* of the Lord in 1 Thessalonians 4:15–17, every believer would have immediately understood the imagery. The "coming of our Lord" wasn't a single moment—it was a process with two distinct parts.

So when Paul said, "We who are alive and remain until the coming [*parousia*] of the Lord . . . shall be caught up together with them in the clouds to meet the Lord in the air" (vv. 15, 17), he was talking about phase one. That word "meet" is *apantesis* in Greek.[6] It's the same word for that welcome committee going out to greet the king.

The rapture (or "catching up") is basically the *apantesis* part of Christ's *parousia*, or coming. We go out to meet Him in the air, just like those ancient welcome committees went out to meet their king. But the *parousia* isn't done until phase two—when we come back with Him.

This is why the rapture and the second coming can be the same event but also different moments. They're like two parts of one *parousia* process, with time in between—just like those ancient royal visits had a gap between the meeting and the final arrival.

Once you understand this cultural context, some of those confusing passages make way more sense. Take 2 Thessalonians 2, where Paul was basically addressing the timing question head-on: "Concerning the coming [*parousia*] of our Lord Jesus Christ and our gathering together to Him . . . that Day will not come unless the falling away comes first, and the man of sin is revealed" (vv. 1, 3). Here's the thing—Paul was saying we can't be raptured until after the Antichrist shows up. He was saying the *parousia*—that whole two-part process we just talked about—won't be completely finished until after these events happen. The first phase (where we get gathered to Him) can happen, but the entire process isn't wrapped up until the final phase when we go back with Him.

Jesus reinforced the timing of the first phase of the *parousia* in Matthew 24:29–31: "Immediately after the tribulation . . . they will see the Son of Man coming on the clouds . . . He will send His angels with a great sound of a trumpet, and they will gather together His elect." Notice that same Greek word for "gathering" shows up here, too, and Jesus appears to clearly express that this happens after the tribulation, not before.

Satan's Tantrum vs. God's Judgment

Okay, but what about all the wrath? If 1 Thessalonians 5 is pretty clear that we're not appointed to God's wrath, how do we reconcile that when we think about the tribulation period? Here's an interesting thought—what if the tribulation period isn't actually God's wrath at work but Satan's?

When you dig into Revelation 12 and 13, it seems clear that the seven-year tribulation is Satan losing his absolute mind, not God dropping judgment. The Scriptures say the dragon literally makes war with people "who keep the commandments of God and have the testimony of Jesus" (Revelation 12:17). That's Satan's tantrum, not God's wrath. God's wrath doesn't show up until later, specifically in the Seven Bowls Judgement (Revelation 16) where God pours out plagues on the earth and culminating in the battle of Armageddon (Revelation 16:16, 19:11–21) where Christ returns to beat the Antichrist and his armies in a final confrontation.

Throughout Scripture we read about faith heroes like Paul, Peter, and John the Baptist spreading the gospel in the hardest of times. A faith that endured persecution and sparked revival beyond their wildest imagination. What if the tribulation is just the ultimate version of that? What if instead of bailing before things get intense, we're called to be the light when everything goes dark?

Because honestly? When the world is falling apart, that's when the church has historically done its most epic work. Signs, wonders, revival that shakes nations, all of it happening right in the middle of Satan's worst tantrum.

All that wrath talk introduced a lot of things that may have taken you for a loop. You could probably write a whole series of books on some of the topics from the past few paragraphs alone. The greatest hour of the church may not be in our escape from the storm but in our faithfulness within it.

Preparing for Escape or Endurance?

You might be asking, "Why does any of this matter? Just let me be raptured in peace!" It matters because how we interpret prophecy shapes how we prepare. If we're overly confident that we'll be out of here before anything gets tough, we may not spiritually prepare to stand firm when it does. But if we understand that God may call us to endure, to shine in darkness, and to stand in the tension, we'll build a stronger, deeper kind of faith. So, here's the friction: Are we preparing our hearts for escape, or for endurance?

We should not approach these truths with fear but with sober hope and readiness. Romans 13 reminds us: "Knowing the time . . . it is high time to awake . . . for now our salvation is nearer than when we first believed" (v. 11). Our response to prophetic fulfillment should be active and vigilant living, casting off darkness and embracing the light.

Ultimately, the signs of Christ's imminent return are clear. The biblical evidence is overwhelming, inviting us to live ready, informed, and discerning lives. Our awareness of prophetic seasons empowers us not only to endure coming challenges but to lead many others to Christ, fulfilling God's purpose in these final days. Think about it. God trusted you to live during the times that we're in now. So many biblical things seem to be unfolding right before our eyes. Things that many believers are likely unaware of. The more certain passages come to life, the harder it becomes not to wonder, *Are these the moments?* Ezekiel 38 and 39 could be pointing to what is transpiring around the world, specifically in the Middle East. The nations mentioned in the Scriptures, which are modern-day Iran, Russia, Turkey, and others, are beginning to team up in real time.[7] Current events continue to be potentially mirroring Scripture. Talks of peace, talks of nations joining forces—it's all there. It's important that the Word of God be our north star in this season.

Hope in Tribulation

Although tribulation signifies immense trials, Scripture also promises profound purification and victory for the church. Daniel 11:32–35 and Revelation 6 describe tribulation as a period of refining and sanctifying believers, much like Israel's protection in Goshen, the area of Egypt where the Israelites lived and were kept safe by God amid Egypt's plagues. God's promise remains firm: His wrath targets evil, not His faithful children. Concerning the day of the Lord, Scripture says that "God did not appoint us to wrath, but to obtain salvation through our Lord Jesus Christ" (1 Thessalonians 5:9). What better time to pursue a relationship with God? When chaos hits, we can hold fast to the promises of the Lord.

Moreover, Jesus' parable of the wheat and tares (Matthew 13) illustrates God separating believers during a harvest. Could this be reinforcing that God's protection and discernment will cover His people during these turbulent times?

So while we can't pinpoint the exact day and hour, Scripture provides abundant clues to help us discern the prophetic season of Christ's return. More than dates and debates, God calls us to live vigilant, purified lives, confidently anticipating our ultimate redemption with joyful hope.

CHAPTER 13

HOW DO WE TURN PROPHECY TO PRACTICE?

From Curiosity into Consecrated Rhythms

Have you finished that latte yet? The pages of this book could have easily equated to several coffee shop conversations. Honestly? We're still trying to figure out how four regular people ended up researching red heifers after visiting a Texas ranch. But here we are, and we wouldn't trade it for anything.

We showed up where God told us to—a cattle ranch in Rockwall, Texas—and the next thing we knew, we were watching history unfold between fence posts and feed buckets. What started as a trip to see some cows turned into a front-row seat to prophecy in motion. Those moments weren't just significant; they were sacred. And they marked us forever. We weren't just documenting an event: We were witnessing the search of the first domino of major prophetic events. The domino that could set everything else in motion.

So now we keep studying. Keep asking questions. And keep

letting God use our curiosity as a compass back to Him and His plans. Every headline feels different now. Every Middle East conflict carries more weight. Every sign of the times feels more urgent, more real, more *now*.

Maybe you're part of this wild ride too. Maybe you're the kind that sees breadcrumbs in the headlines and wonders what's really going on behind the scenes. Maybe you picked up this book skeptical and you're leaving it shaken. Not by fear but by the realization that we might be living in the times Jesus warned us about.

Here's what we've learned: God doesn't waste His invitations. He invited us to a ranch. He's invited you into this conversation. Neither was an accident. So stay curious. Stay ready. Stay in the Word. Keep your eyes on Jesus. Sometimes the most prophetic ground isn't halfway around the world in an ancient holy site; it's right under your feet, in the most ordinary places.

If this book felt like sitting through a prophetic thriller—red heifers, temples, beasts, and all—you might be stepping out of these pages like someone leaving a movie theater midday: squinting into the light, low-key disoriented, wondering what day it is and trying to mentally reboot. Maybe your faith is on fire. Maybe your theology feels like it just took a karate chop to the throat. Maybe you want to karate chop us, although we think that group of people probably didn't make it this far. And maybe you're wrestling with hurt, questions, or that uneasy feeling of "what now?"

Wherever you land, please hear this: We are praying for you. Seriously. And we believe God is with you in the middle of it all and He is drawing you closer to Him. In these final pages, we want to offer a few practical, grounded steps to help you walk forward, not in fear or anxiousness but in confidence, clarity, and deep dependence on our Lord and Savior Jesus Christ. Because no matter how wild the story gets, He's still the center of it all. He will always be the center of it all. We should always keep our eyes on Jesus, the real Author of our book on faith.

But here's what we need you to know: This isn't just about knowing more; it's about surrender. We urge you to lay it all before the Lord. Every question, fear, teaching, theology, opinion, doubt, or detail—bring it to Him. Ask Him to speak. Draw near and let Him guide you. Trust Him fully with your life, even the parts you don't understand yet.

We say this with love and urgency: Deception is rising, even within the church. And we fear that many are falling for clever lies dressed as light. Our desire is to see the church not asleep or confused but burning with truth and power, ready to set captives free when chaos breaks loose, not paralyzed by false teaching or swept away by fear.

But hear us on this: None of us is above being deceived. Each one of us must walk in humility, recognizing that if we believe deception can happen to anyone but us, we're already vulnerable. Our culture is saturated with lies, distractions, and distortions. And if we're not daily surrendering to the Lord, even those who genuinely love Him can get caught in the undertow of confusion. Jesus loves to meet us in a heart posture of humility, not an ego-driven religious performance. He's not impressed by how much we think we know but by how much we're willing to surrender. Humility makes space for truth. It invites His presence, His correction, and His love to shape us from the inside out.

And this is why we care so deeply. Not just about what you know but about who you become in response to Him. We care about your soul. You were made for this moment in history, and we want to see you walk out your God-given assignment, not half awake, not on the sidelines, but fully alive in Christ.

So before you move on, we want to invite you to slow down. Don't just skim or read through this chapter like any other content; pause and really sit with it. Grab your journal, open your Bible, and ask the Holy Spirit to speak. What comes next isn't just more information; it's an invitation. We'll walk through several spiritual practices that are vital for the days we're living in. You'll find encouragement, understanding, and practical steps to help you live awake, grounded, and surrendered.

These rhythms aren't about striving; they're about abiding. They're meant to strengthen your spirit, renew your mind, and align your heart with the One who holds it all. So take time to self-assess, take notes, and let these truths shape your daily walk. Let this be the beginning of a new rhythm, one rooted in eternity, anchored in Christ, and empowered by His Spirit.

Keep Your Eyes on Eternity: Living with the End in Mind

Let's be honest, when the world feels like it's on fire, it's easy to get caught up in the chaos. Headlines, hashtags, and hot takes can flood our minds faster than we can process them. Emotions flare, fears rise, and if we're not careful, our feelings can start driving the car while truth is stuffed in the trunk. But feelings, while real, are not always reliable. If left unchecked and unsubmitted to the Holy Spirit, they can lead us into anxiety, distraction, or even deception. As followers of Jesus, we're called to zoom out and look not just up but within—into the holy ground of His Spirit dwelling in us. The kingdom of heaven isn't just "out there" somewhere. It lives within the walls of our surrendered hearts. Eternity, not urgency, is what should shape our lives. And yet, the urgency is real. The days are short and now is the time to truly challenge yourself to declutter your spiritual vision.

Living with the end in mind doesn't mean we check out or live in constant panic. It means we prioritize what actually matters. Jesus told us in Matthew 6:33 to "seek first the kingdom of God," not just as a spiritual suggestion but as a daily reordering of our heart postures. This is spiritual decluttering. It's asking, "What's taking up space in my life that doesn't matter in light of eternity?" That could be toxic relationships, anxious striving, or just mindless distractions that numb us instead of nourish us.

> Eternity, not urgency, is what should shape our lives.

Paul reminded us in Colossians 3:2 to "set your minds on things above, not on earthly things" (NIV). When we fix our gaze on Jesus and the forever-kingdom we're part of, our temporary struggles shrink back into perspective. We stop building empires of comfort and start investing in what lasts: people, love, truth, obedience, and faith.

So let go of the noise and numbing distractions that dull your awareness of God's voice, and reorder your life around kingdom priorities. Ask yourself: *What am I giving my attention, affection, and energy to? Is it eternal?* The more we let go of what doesn't last, the more room we make for the One who does.

Practically speaking, this can look like:

- **Less** doomscrolling, **more** time in the Word of God.
- **Less** people-pleasing, **more** God-fearing.

- **Less** cluttered calendars, **more** margin to hear His voice.
- **Less** podcast opinions (yes, even *Faith and Friction*), **more** time actually praying.
- **Less** comparison on social media, **more** contentment in Christ.
- **Less** entertainment to "unwind," **more** worship to reset your soul.
- **Less** fear of missing out, **more** joy in missing what doesn't matter.

This isn't about doing more; it's about choosing better. Small, faithful shifts in focus can have a massive impact over time. You don't have to have it all figured out, just start somewhere. God honors your desire to draw near. Let eternity anchor your decisions, your prayers, and your relationships. Jesus is coming back, and we want to be found faithful, not frantic.

PRAYER

Lord, help me to see with eternal eyes. Help me see what You see. Teach me how to clear out the clutter in my heart and mind. The distractions, the fears, the things that pull me away from You. I repent for turning my attention on things that hurt my soul and put distance between us. Teach me to submit my emotions to Your truth and to live from the kingdom within me. Help me reorder my priorities so that my life reflects what matters most to You. Keep me awake, anchored, and aligned with heaven. In Jesus' name, amen.

Don't Panic. Prepare: Becoming Spiritually Resilient

Let's clear something up right away: Preparing for the end times doesn't exclusively mean stockpiling canned goods, toilet paper, and radiation pills, all while googling underground bunkers and blueprints with bowling alleys (although being wise with resources isn't a bad thing and some people are called to prep the land). But real preparation starts with our hearts. What if we hoarded stuff less and pursued holiness more?

Spiritual resilience is about being rooted when everything else feels shaky. It's about having a heart that knows how to stand, not in your own strength but in God's. And the good news? Scripture gives us some incredibly practical ways to build that kind of inner strength.

Prayer

This isn't just a checkbox; it's an actual lifeline. Prayer keeps our hearts aligned with God's. It softens us, strengthens us, and sensitizes us to the Holy Spirit. It can be a whisper, a cry, a song, or silence, but it must be real. Don't wait for perfect words. Just show up.

Fasting

We often think of fasting as an optional extra-credit activity, but in Scripture, it's a regular rhythm for recalibration. Fasting teaches us to say no to our flesh so we can say a louder yes to God. It breaks dependency on the world and reawakens our hunger for heaven. We'd also highly encourage you to take a personal inventory of what is stealing your attention most and fast it monthly, maybe even weekly. Here are some things you can fast to break distraction and recenter your soul.

Digital Fasts:

- Social media
- Streaming platforms
- Podcasts
- News
- Phone-scrolling times

Comfort and Convenience:

- Caffeine or coffee
- Snacking or sugar
- Takeout or fast food
- Shopping (online or in person)

Mental and Emotional Space:

- People-pleasing behaviors (saying no intentionally to protect your spiritual margin)
- Self-criticism or comparison (journal and replace with Scripture truth)
- Constant noise (music, TV, background chatter—replace with silence or worship)

Time and Routine:

- Sleeping in an hour later (fasting that time to pray instead)
- Evening screen time (trade for evening Scripture meditation or worship walk)
- Busywork or overscheduling (fast from saying yes to everything)

Fasting is less about subtraction and more about creating sacred space to hear, obey, and enjoy God. Each month, ask:

What is pulling my attention from Jesus right now? Then lay it down for a few days or a week and let the hunger lead you to Him.

Studying Scripture

If you're not grounded in the Word, you're vulnerable to anything that sounds good but isn't God. This is not the time for secondhand faith. Deception isn't just coming from the world; it can show up in the church, too, wrapped in charisma, tradition, or even partial truth. That's why your personal relationship with Christ really matters. Knowing *about* God isn't the same as *knowing* Him. We need to be anchored in what God actually says, so when deception creeps in (and it will), we're not easily swayed. Even a few verses a day, read slowly and with intention, can anchor your soul more than you realize.

Cultivating Discernment

In a world of half-truths and spiritual counterfeits, discernment is a must. How do you grow it? Stay close to God's Word, listen to His Spirit, and surround yourself with wise, mature believers. Discernment isn't about paranoia. It's about clarity. It's learning to ask: Is this from God, or just dressed up like it is?

Community

You weren't meant to do this alone. God designed us to grow, wrestle, and walk in truth together. Being part of a healthy, Jesus-centered community means you're encouraged when you're weary, equipped when you're unsure, and lovingly challenged when you're drifting.

Community sharpens us, holds us accountable, and reminds us of what's true when we forget. Especially in days of deception and division, walking in unity with other believers isn't optional, it's essential.

So yes, prepare. But prepare the kind of life that can stand firm in love, walk in truth, and shine with peace when everything else feels dark. Because resilience isn't found in what you've stored up in your pantry, but in what you've stored up in your heart.

PRAYER

Jesus, I don't want to panic. I want to prepare my heart. I want to stand firm on Your foundation. I want to trust You fully. Teach me to pursue holiness over hype. Help me to make prayer my first instinct, not my last resort. Give me the discipline to fast, the hunger to seek You in Scripture, and the courage to obey what You show me. Sharpen my discernment so I can recognize Your voice above all others. And surround me with a godly community. People who will encourage me, challenge me, and walk with me in truth and love. Make me resilient, not by my own strength but through Your Spirit alive in me. I want to be ready, not just for what's coming but for whatever You call me to today. In Jesus' name, amen.

Get Anchored in Truth

While we briefly touched on this earlier, it's important enough to stand on its own, because in a world swirling with confusion and counterfeit truth, being anchored in God's Word isn't just helpful; it's essential.

Let's keep it real: We are swimming, drowning, really, in opinions, philosophies, TikTok theology, and spirituality that sounds inspiring but doesn't hold water. We're in an age where lies don't just show up in obvious ways. They're often half true, emotionally compelling, and dressed in light. If you're not anchored in truth, you'll be tossed by every trending revelation or viral video that claims to be from God but contradicts His Word.

And one of the biggest lies gaining traction right now is that the Bible can't be trusted. That it's outdated, man-made, full of contradictions, or culturally irrelevant. These narratives are subtle but dangerous, because if the Enemy can get you to doubt the authority of Scripture, everything else starts to unravel. If the Bible isn't true, then who defines truth? If it's just a suggestion, then Jesus becomes optional. But the Bible isn't just ink on paper—it's the living, God-breathed truth that reveals who He is, who we are, and what's real.

This is why biblical literacy isn't just a nice goal; it's a survival skill. It's the difference between recognizing a counterfeit and falling for it. God's Word is not just a history book or a theological manual. It's your sword, your anchor, your daily bread, and your filter for reality. You can't follow Jesus closely if you're fuzzy on what He actually said.

But this isn't just about knowing Scripture. It's also about loving it. Falling in love with God's Word means you're not just mining it for facts but meeting a person. Jesus is the Word made flesh. When you open your Bible, you're learning *and* you're encountering, whether you feel it or not. And over time, that Word gets inside you. It renews your mind, protects your heart, and strengthens your spirit.

You don't have to read the whole Bible in a year, although there are some incredible Bible reading plans out there. Start small but go deep. Read slowly. Ask questions. Let the Holy Spirit guide you into truth. Use a study Bible. Listen to it on your walk. Join a Bible study group. Whatever it takes, get rooted. Because when the storms hit (and they will), it's God's truth that will hold you. Not vibes. Not hype. Him.

And please hear us when we say this: If someone has used Scripture, or the name of Jesus, to control, wound, or manipulate you, we are truly sorry. They are not God. They are human—flawed, fallen, and in some cases, hurting people who hurt others. Hear us loud and clear: That was not Christ. That was not His heart, His character, or His way. We grieve with you for the pain that may have been done in His name, and we pray you'll find the courage to forgive—not to excuse what happened but so your heart can be freed from the weight of it. Forgiveness doesn't mean forgetting; it means choosing to release the offense so that you can step into the healing, truth, and freedom that only Jesus Himself can give.

PRAYER

"In the beginning was the Word, and the Word was with God, and the Word was God" (John 1:1). Lord, we're in awe that the same Word that spoke creation into existence is still alive and active today. Thank You that Your Word isn't just ancient text; it's living, breathing, and powerful. In a world full of noise and confusion, help me tune my heart to Your truth. Give me a hunger for Scripture, a desire not just to read it but to live it. Teach me to recognize Your voice on every page and to build my life on what is eternal, not what is trending. Strengthen my faith, deepen my understanding, and anchor my soul in You. In Jesus' name, amen.

Set Apart, Not Checked Out: Holiness Without Hiding

Let's keep it real: It's tempting to check out. To throw your phone in a drawer, move to the mountains, homeschool your chickens, and avoid culture altogether. And while a quiet life with less noise is definitely a gift in today's world, holiness is not the same as hiding.

Yes, we are called to be set apart. To live differently, think differently, love differently. But set apart doesn't mean spiritually quarantined. Jesus didn't hide from the world. He entered it fully, but He was never of it. He dined with sinners, spoke truth to power, and engaged the brokenness of humanity without ever compromising His holiness. And now, we're called to walk that same line.

Holiness means refusing to be shaped by the values of the world while still being present in it with compassion, boldness, and love. It's not about legalism or perfection; it's about allegiance. It's about saying, "Jesus gets the final word on how I live, how I think, and how I love." It's the daily, often quiet decision to live for an audience of One, even when it's uncomfortable, unpopular, or misunderstood.

Being set apart might look like walking away from gossip at work, choosing contentment when comparison screams louder, or holding the line on purity, honesty, and generosity when culture says, "Do whatever makes you happy." It's not about blending in, but it's also not about being weird for the sake of being weird. It's about influence. Light in darkness. Salt in a flavorless world. A steady presence that reflects Jesus without shouting over people.

And let's be honest, living this way can feel costly. In fact, it will absolutely cost you something. You might feel lonely at times. Misunderstood. Even mocked. But Scripture says you're blessed when you're persecuted for righteousness' sake (Matthew 5:10). You're not alone. You're following in the footsteps of every faithful believer who's chosen the narrow path.

Don't check out. Don't hide your light. Stay soft. Stay bold. Stay anchored. Let holiness be your witness, not in a holier-than-thou kind of way but in a "something about your life looks like heaven" kind of way.

PRAYER

Jesus, help me stay checked in and teach me how to walk in holiness without hiding, to reflect Your love without compromising truth. Give me courage to stand firm when the pressure to blend in feels overwhelming. Keep my heart soft, my convictions strong, and my presence full of grace. May my life be a light that draws others to You, not because I'm perfect but because You are. Use me to bring hope, truth, and love. In a world that's desperate for something real, let me live in a way that makes heaven hard to ignore. In Jesus' name, amen.

Faith over Fear: Hearing God's Voice in the Storm

When life gets loud, learning to hear God's voice isn't just helpful, it's crucial. We're not just trying to survive the storm, we're learning to walk through it with clarity, courage, and calmness. But to do that, we need to know who's speaking.

Fear has a voice. So does culture. So does your flesh. But none of those voices can lead you like the Holy Spirit can. His voice brings peace, not panic. Conviction, not condemnation. Clarity, not confusion. And when you learn to recognize His voice, it anchors your faith even when everything around you is shaking.

This kind of spiritual listening doesn't happen by accident. It's cultivated: quietly, daily, intentionally. It looks like making space to be still, to pray, to open your Bible and ask God to speak through it. It means pausing before reacting, checking in with the Spirit before checking your feed, and training your heart to listen more than you speak. The Holy Spirit isn't hiding; He's just not shouting over your chaos.

And here's the beauty: The more time you spend with someone, the more you recognize their voice. The same is true with God. The more you walk with Him, the less power fear has over you. Because instead of asking, "What if everything falls apart?" you start asking, "What is God saying right now?" That's how peace begins to win.

Fear will always try to take the mic in uncertain times, but as believers, we get to turn the volume down on fear and tune in to the voice of our Shepherd. He's still speaking. The question is: Are you listening? Fear will try to lead you into spiraling over everything related to the last days. It'll try to grip your peace in a way that leads to overwhelming uncertainty. Whose theology is accurate? When are we being raptured? Will I be persecuted? How can I know I hear God's voice? Can I accidentally take the mark of the beast? When should I start stockpiling my pantry?

Those questions might feel like a lot, but they're honest and you're not alone in asking them. The good news is that you have the power to pause the panic. Scripture reminds us that God hasn't given us a spirit of fear but of power, love, and a sound mind (2 Timothy 1:7). And that sound mind anchors us both in the conversation and in confidence in Jesus for the days ahead.

PRAYER

God, when the world is loud and my heart feels overwhelmed, help me hear You. Teach me to recognize Your voice above the noise of fear, anxiety, and confusion. Quiet every voice that doesn't lead me closer to Your heart. Give me ears to hear what the Spirit is saying and a heart that responds with faith, not fear. Train me to pause, to listen, and to follow, especially when things feel uncertain. Thank You that You're not a distant God but a present Shepherd, leading me with peace and truth. I choose to trust Your voice in the storm. In Jesus' name, amen.

The Remnant Rising: You're Not Alone

If you've ever felt like the odd one out for following Jesus in a world that seems to be sprinting in the opposite direction, you're not crazy, and you're definitely not alone. It might feel like you're standing by yourself, but the truth is that God always preserves a remnant.

All throughout Scripture, when things looked bleak, when culture was crumbling, when idolatry was running rampant, when compromise was the norm, God still had a faithful few. Quiet ones. Courageous ones. People who refused to bow to the world and kept their eyes fixed on Him. Friend, that's you. That's us.

You don't have to wait for the world to get it together before you walk in purpose. The world might never get it together. But we were born for such a time as this (Esther 4:14). This isn't about surviving the storm; it's about rising in the middle of it, as light bearers, truth tellers, disciple makers, and kingdom builders.

That means plugging into a community that strengthens your faith—people who sharpen you, hold you accountable, encourage your calling, and pull you back to truth when you drift. Isolation is a breeding ground for fear and compromise, but community keeps your fire burning.

It also means investing in others—discipling, mentoring, encouraging—even if you feel like you're still figuring things out yourself (spoiler: We all are). There's someone behind you who needs what you've learned, and someone ahead of you who can help you keep going.

So don't shrink back. This is not the time to go quiet. The

remnant is rising. Not because we're impressive but because we serve a God who moves through the humble, the willing, and the surrendered. You were made for now. You were called for here. You are not alone. You're part of the remnant.

PRAYER

God, thank You for never leaving us to stand alone. When the world feels like it's spinning out of control, remind me that You are preserving a faithful remnant . . . Your people. Help me find my place in a community where I can be encouraged, challenged, and equipped. Give me the courage to disciple others, knowing that even in my weakness, Your strength is made perfect. Use me to shine Your light in this dark season and to stand firm in the calling You've placed on my life. May I never forget: I'm not alone, and I'm here for such a time as this. In Jesus' name, amen.

Intercession: How to Intercede in the Last Days

Prayer isn't just a spiritual safety net or a quick "Dear God, fix this" before bed. No, prayer in these times is powerful, active, and strategic. It's how we partner with God to push back against darkness, confusion, and chaos. Think of it like spiritual warfare, fought with faith-filled words and persistent hearts.

The last days can feel overwhelming. There's so much to pray about: brokenness everywhere, deception swirling, and the world's moral compass spinning wildly. But here's the truth: Your prayers matter. They are not wasted breath. They move heaven and earth.

Start by praying for Israel, the heartbeat of biblical prophecy and God's chosen people. The Bible tells us to pray for peace in Jerusalem (Psalm 122:6). Yet, with ongoing wars and a flood of conflicting narratives swirling around the region, many believers feel confused or uncertain about how, and even for whom, to pray. But when we lift up Israel, we align ourselves with God's redemptive plan, trusting His promises beyond the noise and the headlines. At the same time, we can, and should, pray compassionately for all those affected by war: families torn apart, refugees displaced, and innocent lives caught in the crossfire. God's heart is for peace and healing for all people, and our prayers can be a powerful channel of His mercy.

Next, ask God for wisdom, not just for yourself but for leaders, pastors, and anyone walking in influence. We desperately need godly insight to navigate these turbulent times without falling into fear or deception.

Prayer is also where we ask for boldness, to speak truth with love, to stand firm in our faith, and to share the gospel even when it's risky or unpopular.

And don't forget to pray against deception and lawlessness. The Bible warns us about the rise of lies and moral decay in the last days, but prayer is a weapon that cuts through the darkness. We can plead for clarity, protection, and for God's kingdom to advance.

This kind of prayer moves us from passivity to purpose. It reminds us that we're not helpless spectators but active participants in God's story. So instead of waiting for change, let's pray for change and watch how God moves through our faith-filled petitions.

PRAYER

Lord, we come before You not in fear but in faith, believing that You've positioned us in this moment for a purpose. Teach us to pray with precision and power. Give us Your heart for Israel, and help us lift up Your people with love and understanding, even in the middle of confusion and war.

Grant us wisdom in a world clouded with lies. Help us discern truth from deception, both in culture and within the church. Make us bold, not passive. Help us stand firm in truth and speak with compassion, even when it's costly.

We pray against the spirit of lawlessness that seeks to divide and deceive. Instead, fill us with Your Spirit so we may partner with You to push back darkness and proclaim Your kingdom with power.

Let our prayers be our first response, not our last resort. Make us intercessors who contend with heaven and move the needle of history, not by might or power but by Your Spirit. In Jesus' name, amen.

Worship as Warfare: Keeping Our Hearts Aligned

Worship isn't just about singing the right songs on Sunday mornings or having a killer playlist for your commute.

Worship is a posture, a lifestyle of surrender that keeps our hearts tuned to God's frequency, no matter what storms rage around us.

When we worship, we're pushing back against fear, anxiety, and heaviness. Praise has the power to silence the lies whispering in our minds and break the chains of despair holding us down. It's spiritual warfare with our voices and our hearts.

Worship is a posture, a lifestyle of surrender that keeps our hearts tuned to God's frequency, no matter what storms rage around us.

Worship shifts our focus from the chaos of the world to the unshakable goodness of God. It aligns us with His heart, reminding us of who He is and who we are in Him. When fear wants to take the driver's seat, worship gently takes it back, steering us toward peace.

And here's the cool part: Worship isn't just for the mountaintops or when things are going great. It's for the valleys, the battles, and the waiting seasons too. It's how we keep our souls anchored and our faith fierce. So wherever you are, whatever you're facing, worship is your weapon and your refuge. Don't just sing it but live it. When you're taken aback by a headline or report you see in the days, weeks, and years to come, take it as an invitation to worship. To connect with the Spirit of God that offers peace and comfort. Because in the uncertainty of the last days, worship reminds us who's really on the throne, and that no matter what unfolds, we belong to a kingdom that cannot be shaken.

PRAYER

Father, You are worthy of all praise, whether my heart is soaring or heavy. Teach me to worship You beyond the songs and rituals, to live in surrender every moment. When fear tries to creep in, remind me to lift my voice and focus on Your goodness. Let my praise break chains, silence lies, and align me with Your heart. Help me to worship not just on Sundays but in the daily grind, battles, and waiting. May my life be a constant act of worship, pushing back darkness and drawing me closer to You. In Jesus' name, amen.

Jesus: The Center of It All

Let's take a deep breath together. After pages of prophecy, signs, symbols, temples, beasts, wars, and timelines, here's what matters most: Jesus.

Not the red heifer.

Not the Third Temple.

Not even the Antichrist.

And definitely not the tribulation.

None of these get the spotlight. Jesus does. Always. He's the Alpha and the Omega, the beginning, the end, and everything in between. Every prophecy points to Him. Every headline should turn our eyes toward Him. Every moment of confusion or urgency is just another chance to anchor our hearts in His unchanging truth.

It's so easy to get sidetracked, even with good intentions. We want to figure it out, map the timeline, and predict the signs. But the goal isn't just information, it's transformation. And that only happens when we're face-to-face with Christ.

Jesus is not a side character in Revelation. He's the Lamb who was slain and the King who returns in glory. He is our blessed hope. Our Savior, Redeemer, Bridegroom, and Judge. And He's not far off. He's near, and He's coming soon.

So as we wrap up this journey, we invite you: Fix your gaze on Him. Let everything else fade into the background noise. Don't build your life on speculation. Build it on Jesus, the solid rock who never fails.

PRAYER

Jesus, You are the center of it all. Not prophecy, not politics, not fear . . . You. Forgive us for the ways we've made it about signs and missed the Savior. You are the Lamb who died and the King who's coming back. Help us keep our hearts anchored in You, our eyes fixed on You, and our lives surrendered to You. Let every question drive us closer to Your presence. Let every moment of wonder lead to deeper worship. And until You return, help us live in love, in truth, and in step with You. In Your holy, powerful name, amen.

GLOSSARY

144,000—A prophetic group mentioned in Revelation 7 and 14, consisting of 12,000 individuals from each of the twelve tribes of Israel, sealed by God during the tribulation for protection and as a sign of His covenant faithfulness to Israel. Some interpret their role as evangelistic, others as symbolic of Israel's restoration.

88 Reasons Why the Rapture Will Be in 1988—A self-published book by former NASA engineer, Edgar C. Whisenant, that gained popularity for attempting to calculate the rapture date using biblical numerology. It is now commonly referenced as an example of failed eschatological prediction.

1948 (establishment of Israel)—The year modern Israel became an independent nation. This marked the beginning of renewed efforts by Jews to reclaim and fulfill various prophetic and religious mandates, such as seeking the red heifer.

A

Aaronic priesthood—The hereditary priesthood that originated with Aaron. Priests (*Kohanim*) from this line were given special responsibilities in the temple, including offerings and purification rites.

"Abomination of desolation"—A phrase Jesus used (Matthew 24:15) referring to a future desecration of the holy place (likely the temple). Many believe it has a future prophetic fulfillment by the Antichrist.

Abrahamic covenant—The foundational promise God made to Abraham in Genesis 12 and reaffirmed and ratified in Genesis 15 and 17. It includes blessings, land, descendants, and the promise that all nations of the earth would be blessed through his seed. It is an everlasting covenant that forms the basis for God's relationship with Israel.

Al-Aqsa Mosque—One of the holiest sites in Islam, located on the Temple Mount. The presence of the mosque is believed to complicate efforts to rebuild the Jewish temple, making the site a flash point of religious and political conflict.

Alliance of ten kings / ten horns—Referenced in Daniel 7 and Revelation 13, symbolic of a ten-nation coalition from which the Antichrist will rise, overthrowing three and gaining power.

Amillennialists—Those that believe the one thousand years are symbolic and happening now.

Antichrist—A future political or spiritual leader who will oppose Christ, deceive the nations, and exalt himself as divine (2 Thessalonians 2; Revelation 13). Some see him as a person; others see the term more symbolically or spiritually.

Antiochus IV Epiphanes—A second-century BC Seleucid king who persecuted Jews and desecrated the temple. Often viewed as a prophetic type and shadow of the Antichrist.

Ark of the covenant—A sacred gold-covered chest described in the Old Testament, containing the stone tablets of the Ten Commandments. Represented God's throne on earth. Its exact location remains unknown, but discovery would have monumental religious and prophetic implications.

Armageddon—From Har Megiddo ("Mount Megiddo"), it's believed to be the site of the final battle between good and evil before Christ's return (Revelation 16:16). It's both literal and symbolic in interpretation depending on the theology.

Assyrian Exile (722 BC)—The conquest of the Northern Kingdom of Israel by Assyria, leading to the dispersion and loss of ten tribes. Commonly referred to as the "lost tribes of Israel."

Atonement of sins (Judaism vs. Christianity)—In Judaism, especially pre-Christ, atonement was achieved through temple sacrifices. In Christianity, Jesus' death on the cross is viewed as the final atonement for all sins, making future sacrifices unnecessary for salvation.

B

Babylonian exile—The period when the Babylonians conquered Judah, destroyed Solomon's temple, and carried the Jewish people into exile. Marked a major turning point in Israel's prophetic and historical story.

Bar Kokhba Revolt—A Jewish rebellion led by Simon bar Kokhba against Roman rule around AD 132–135. Though initially successful, it was crushed by the Romans, resulting in devastating consequences for the Jewish people, including exile from Jerusalem.

Blindness/hardening in part—Described in Romans 11:25, it refers to a partial, temporary spiritual blindness over the Jewish people in recognizing Jesus as the Messiah, which will be lifted in God's timing when the "fullness of the Gentiles" comes in.

C

Ceremonial uncleanness—A temporary state under Old Testament law that prevented someone from participating in religious activities, often caused by things like touching a dead body. Rituals like the red heifer sacrifice were used to restore "clean" status.

Cherubim—Heavenly beings described as guardians of God's presence. Far from the baby-angel depiction, biblical cherubim have multiple wings, faces, and are associated with worship and divine protection (Ezekiel 1; Revelation 4).

Chronos—A Greek word referring to chronological or sequential time. Measurable units like hours, days, and years. Paul used this term in 1 Thessalonians 5 to describe linear time.

Copper Scroll—A literal copper document found in Qumran's Cave 3 listing locations of buried temple treasures, including gold, silver, and vessels. Some believe it may point to the location of the ark of the covenant or other temple artifacts. Scholars debate the treasure's reality, its connection to the temple, and the cryptic nature of its inscriptions.

Covenant (biblical)—A divine, binding promise between God and His people. There are several covenants in the Bible, but the Abrahamic covenant is foundational to the story of Israel and the Jewish people.

"Covenant with many" (Daniel 9:27)—A seven-year peace agreement initiated by the Antichrist, likely involving Israel and other nations, which he later breaks midway.

Cutting covenant—An ancient custom where two parties sealed a covenant by walking between animal sacrifices, symbolizing, "May this happen to me if I break this covenant."

D

Daniel's beasts (Daniel 7)—Vision of four beasts representing kingdoms; the final beast has ten horns, out of which a little horn (Antichrist) rises.

Daniel's seventy weeks—A prophecy in Daniel 9 that outlines seventy sets of "weeks" (interpreted as years), believed by many to point to the timing of Jesus' first coming and the events of the end times.

Day of the Lord—A biblical phrase describing a future time of divine intervention, judgment, and the ultimate fulfillment of God's purposes. Associated with both wrath and deliverance.

Deception—A major tactic of the Antichrist involving counterfeit miracles, persuasive rhetoric, and false peace to mislead the world.

Descendants of Aaron—The priestly line in ancient Israel. Aaron, brother of Moses, was the first high priest, and his male descendants were chosen to carry out temple duties, including sacrifices and purification rituals.

Dispensationalism—This is a way that some Christians read the Bible that splits history into "seasons" or "dispensations," where God works with people in different ways. It keeps Israel and the church on separate tracks and sees end times prophecy as a literal future plan that God will roll out step by step.

Divine priority vs. favoritism—A theme developed throughout chapter 5: God's choice of Israel reflects His covenant order, not favoritism. Being "first" means greater responsibility, not superiority.

Division of the kingdom (931 BC)—After King Solomon's reign, the united kingdom of Israel split into the Northern Kingdom (Israel) and the Southern Kingdom (Judah). This division plays a crucial role in the distinction between "Israelites" and "Jews."

Dome of the Rock—An Islamic shrine located on the Temple Mount in Jerusalem. It is one of Islam's holiest sites, believed to be the location of the prophet Muhammad's ascension to heaven. Built on the traditional site of the Jewish temple.

Dragon (Satan)—Described in Revelation 12 and 13 as the power behind the Antichrist and the False Prophet, giving them authority and influence.

E

Ephraim and Manasseh—The two sons of Joseph whom Jacob adopted as his own, effectively giving Joseph a double portion of inheritance among the tribes.

Eschatology—The study of the "last things" or end times, covering death, judgment, heaven, hell, the return of Christ, the resurrection, and the final destiny of humanity.

Exodus—Refers both to the second book of the Bible and the historical event of the Israelites' departure from slavery in Egypt under Moses' leadership. The first red heifer sacrifice is tied to this period in Jewish tradition.

Ezekiel's temple vision—Found in Ezekiel 40–48, this is a detailed prophetic vision of a future temple with precise dimensions, layout, and features. Some interpret it symbolically, but many believe it refers to a literal third temple yet to be built.

Ezra—A priest and scribe in the Old Testament, traditionally credited with preparing the second red heifer during the era of the First Temple's rebuilding. He is known for restoring Jewish worship and law after the Babylonian exile.

F

False Prophet—A secondary end times figure who supports the Antichrist, performs signs, and compels the world to worship the Antichrist (Revelation 13).

Fig tree prophecy—Jesus' teaching in Matthew 24 using a fig tree as a metaphor. When it sprouts leaves, it signals the nearness of summer, just as prophetic signs indicate the closeness of His return.

First Temple—Built by King Solomon in Jerusalem, it was the original permanent structure for Jewish worship. Known for its grandeur and the visible glory of God, it was destroyed by the Babylonians in 586 BC.

Firstborn nation—A biblical concept that Israel was God's "firstborn son" among the nations (Exodus 4:22), indicating both privilege and responsibility in carrying His name and message.

"Fullness of the Gentiles"—A mysterious phrase from Romans 11:25. It refers to the completion of God's plan for Gentiles before the collective turning of Israel back to God.

Interpretations vary on whether this is a number, a time, or a spiritual milestone.

Futurism—An interpretive view of prophecy that holds the position that most of Revelation describes future, literal events, including the rise of the Antichrist and a seven-year tribulation.

G

Gematria—An ancient Jewish system of assigning numerical values to letters, words, or phrases in the Hebrew alphabet. The idea is that since each Hebrew letter corresponds to a number, words with the same numerical value may carry hidden connections or deeper spiritual meaning.

God's faithfulness to Israel—A key theme that God has not abandoned His people, and His covenant with Israel remains active and essential to eschatology.

God's irrevocable covenant—Referencing Romans 11:29, this phrase reminds us that God's promises to Israel, though unfulfilled in part, remain active and will be completed in His timing.

Gog and Magog—Prophetic enemies mentioned in Ezekiel 38–39 and Revelation 20. Some see this as a literal future war, others as symbolic of Satan-led rebellion against God.

Grafted in—A term from Romans 11 describing how Gentile believers are spiritually adopted into the family of God, partaking in the blessings originally given to Israel. They don't replace the Jews but are added to the covenant community.

Great Commission—A command from Jesus in Matthew 28:19–20 instructing believers to go and make disciples of all nations, baptizing them and teaching them His commands. This is the core Christian calling, regardless of prophetic events.

Great tribulation—A future period of intense suffering and persecution, often identified as the last 3.5 years of the 7-year tribulation (Matthew 24:21; Revelation 7:14).

H

Hadrian—A Roman emperor who responded to the Bar Kokhba Revolt by renaming Jerusalem to Aelia Capitolina and Judea to Syria Palestina, effectively erasing Jewish national identity in the region.

Hamas—A Palestinian Islamist militant group. Mentioned in the context of a CBS article discussing their public statements against the red heifers being brought to Israel, framing it as part of a religious or prophetic conflict.

Herod's temple (Second Temple renovation)—An expansion and beautification of Zerubbabel's temple carried out by King Herod. This was the temple Jesus walked into and taught in.

Hilchot Parah Adumah (3:4)—A section of the Mishneh Torah where Maimonides stated that the tenth red heifer will be prepared by the King Messiah, highlighting the prophetic importance of this ritual in Jewish thought.

Historicist view—A prophetic interpretation that views Revelation as an unfolding of church history. Reformers like Luther and Calvin identified the papacy as the Antichrist.

Holy of holies—The innermost and most sacred part of the tabernacle and later the temple, where the ark of the covenant was kept and God's presence dwelled.

I

Idealist view—A nonliteral prophetic interpretation where symbols in Revelation represent timeless truths. The Antichrist is viewed more as a spiritual force or system.

Imam—a person who leads prayers in a mosque and provides spiritual guidance for the Muslim community.

Isaac—The son of Abraham and Sarah. Chosen by God to carry the covenant promise. His lineage, not Ishmael's, is the line through which God's redemptive plan continues.

Ishmael—Abraham's firstborn son through Hagar. Though not the heir of the covenant, God blessed Ishmael and his descendants, who many believe are traditionally linked to many Arab nations.

J

Jacob (Israel)—Son of Isaac, twin of Esau. Renamed "Israel" after wrestling with God (Genesis 32:28). He fathered twelve sons, who became the heads of the twelve tribes of Israel.

Jerusalem Embassy Act (1995)—A US law recognizing Jerusalem as Israel's capital and calling for the US Embassy to be moved there from Tel Aviv. It was enacted in 2018 under President Trump.

Jew—Originally derived from the tribe of Judah. Over time, especially after the Babylonian exile, the term became associated with all Israelites, particularly those from the tribes of Judah, Benjamin, and Levi.

Jewish identity (bloodline)—Biblical Jewish identity is defined by descent from Abraham through Isaac and Jacob.

Jewish oral law—Teachings and interpretations passed down orally by Jewish sages and rabbis, later compiled into texts like the Mishnah and Talmud. These help explain how Jews understood and applied the written Torah.

Jewish Virtual Library—An online resource that compiles information on Jewish history, culture, politics, and religion. Mentioned as a source for tracking red heifer history.

Jonathan Edwards—An eighteenth-century American theologian and preacher known for his revivalist messages during the First Great Awakening. Quoted as someone who lived in a state of constant readiness for the return of Christ.

Judah—One of the twelve sons of Jacob. The tribe of Judah became dominant, and the term Jew originates from Judah. King David and Jesus both come from this tribe.

K

Kairos—A Greek word meaning an appointed or opportune time; a divine moment when God acts. Used in both 1 Thessalonians 5 and Romans 13 to emphasize spiritual readiness.

King Cyrus of Persia—A pagan king who was moved by God to allow the Jews to return from exile and rebuild the temple. Often cited as a Gentile instrument of God's will (Ezra 1).

King Messiah—In Jewish belief, this refers to the promised future anointed king from the line of David who will bring peace, rebuild the temple, and restore Israel. Christians believe Jesus fulfilled this role in His first coming, while many Jews are still waiting for his arrival.

Kosher—From the Hebrew word *kasher*, meaning fit, proper, and acceptable. Something that meets the requirements of Jewish law (*halakah*), especially in relation to food, ritual purity, and sacrificial practice.

L

Levi (tribe of Levi)—One of the twelve tribes of Israel. The Levites were set apart for priestly duties and temple service.

Lost tribes of Israel—The ten northern tribes of Israel that were conquered and scattered by the Assyrian Empire. They disappeared from history as identifiable groups.

M

Man of lawlessness / Antichrist—A figure described in Scripture who will rise to global power, oppose God, deceive many, and declare himself divine. His appearance is a key event in the end-time prophecy.

Mark of the beast—A mark on the right hand or forehead and symbol of allegiance to the Antichrist during the end times. Without it, people cannot buy or sell. Its exact nature is debated but seen as economic and spiritual control (Revelation 13:16–17).

Matthew 24:36 ("no one knows the day or hour")—A commonly quoted verse where Jesus emphasized that no one knows the exact timing of His return, not even angels. However, other passages suggest that believers should still recognize the season and signs.

Messianic Age—A future era anticipated in Jewish thought, marked by peace, justice, and divine reign. For Christians, it begins with Jesus' second coming. For Jews, it's inaugurated by the arrival of their long-awaited messiah.

Messianic Jews—Jewish believers in Jesus (Yeshua) as the Messiah. They retain their Jewish identity while embracing Jesus as the fulfillment of messianic prophecy.

Millennium / millennial kingdom—A one-thousand-year reign of Christ described in Revelation 20.

Mishnah—A foundational Jewish text compiled around AD 200, consisting of oral laws and traditions passed down from earlier generations. It provides commentary and interpretation of the Torah and is a key source for understanding Jewish religious practices.

Mishnah Parah (3:5)—A specific section of the Mishnah that discusses the laws surrounding the red heifer, including historical references to how and when red heifers were prepared for purification.

Mishneh Torah—A fourteen-volume work by Maimonides that organizes and explains Jewish law. It includes a statement about the tenth red heifer being sacrificed by the Messiah, a significant claim in Jewish eschatology.

Moshe ben Maimon (Maimonides)—A twelfth-century Jewish rabbi, philosopher, and legal scholar whose writings continue to influence Jewish thought. Known for his book

Mishneh Torah, a codification of Jewish law, where he discussed the history and future of red heifer sacrifices. His works are foundational in Jewish law and theology. He taught that the tenth red heifer would be sacrificed by the coming Messiah.

Mount Moriah / Threshing floor of Ornan (Araunah)—The traditional site where Solomon built the First Temple, originally the place where David built an altar. Believed to be the true location of the holy of holies.

Mustafa Abu Sway—A contemporary Muslim religious leader (imam at Al-Aqsa) quoted as describing the temple situation as "a Pandora's box nobody can close," highlighting the volatility and religious sensitivity of the area.

N

Nephilim—Mentioned in Genesis 6:4, giants born from the union of fallen angels (sons of God) and human women. Considered by some to be linked spiritually or genetically to the Antichrist.

Nero Caesar—Roman emperor infamous for persecuting Christians. Often cited by preterists as a possible fulfillment of the beast in Revelation.

New Jerusalem—The heavenly city described in Revelation 21–22 where God dwells with His people forever. Seen as the final "reset." No pain, no tears, no death.

Nimrod—A powerful ruler mentioned in Genesis 10, associated with Babylon and the Tower of Babel. Seen by some as an archetype of rebellion and a forerunner to the Antichrist.

Numbers 19—A chapter in the Old Testament that outlines the ritual of sacrificing a red heifer and using its ashes to purify people who have become ceremonially unclean, especially through contact with a dead body.

O

October 7, 2023 (Israel-Hamas Conflict)—The date of a surprise attack by Hamas on Israel that escalated tensions and war in the region. The red heifers were mentioned by Hamas as part of their grievances, showing how religious prophecy can be interwoven into political and military conflict.

Olive tree metaphor (Romans 11)—Paul's illustration of God's covenant people. Israel is the natural olive tree. Some branches (unbelieving Jews) were broken off, and Gentile believers (wild branches) were grafted in. Yet God can graft natural branches back in.

Orthodox Jews—A branch of Judaism that strictly adheres to traditional beliefs and interpretations of the Torah and Jewish law. Orthodox Jews do not accept Jesus as the Messiah and still anticipate a future messianic figure.

P

Pandora's box—A metaphor for something that seems small or insignificant but ends up unleashing large-scale and uncontrollable consequences. Used in chapter 3 to describe the potential conflict surrounding red heifers and temple construction.

Parousia—a Greek word used throughout the New Testament regarding the second coming or "coming of the Lord," meaning "coming" or "arrival." It is culturally a two-part event when a king is entering a city.

Pharaoh's hardened heart—In Exodus 9:12, God "hardened Pharaoh's heart (NIV)." Believed to bring about deliverance through the plagues and call out false Egyptian gods. Paralleled in the New Testament with the concept of God allowing partial spiritual blindness for divine purposes.

Postmillennialists—Believe that Jesus will return after the one thousand years described in Revelation 20.

Premillennialists—Believe Jesus returns before this one-thousand-year reign.

Preterism—A view that many end times prophecies (like Matthew 24 and Revelation) were fulfilled in the first century, especially in the destruction of Jerusalem in AD 70.

Prophetic fulfillment—The idea that certain Old Testament laws, rituals, and symbols (like the red heifer) foreshadow events that are or will be fulfilled in the New Testament, especially related to Jesus and end times.

Purification ritual—A sacred ceremony in the Old Testament designed to cleanse a person from ritual impurity, making them spiritually clean and able to participate in temple worship.

Q

Qumran—An archaeological site near the Dead Sea where the Dead Sea Scrolls were found, including the Copper Scroll.

Believed to have been a settlement of Essenes and possibly priestly custodians of temple treasures.

R

Rapture—The belief that Christians will be "caught up" (raptured) to meet Jesus in the air (1 Thessalonians 4:17). It comes from the Latin word *rapiemur* (to be snatched up), which translates into the Greek word *harpazō*. So when Paul said believers will be "caught up" with Jesus, that's what later Christians started calling the "rapture."

Rebuilt Third Temple—A yet-to-be-constructed temple in Jerusalem that plays a central role in prophecy, especially as the place where the Antichrist will declare himself God (2 Thessalonians 2:4).

Red heifer—A rare, completely red cow without blemish or defect that has never been yoked. Described in Numbers 19, its ashes were used in ancient Israelite purification rituals. Many Jews and some Christians believe a future red heifer will play a role in enabling the rebuilding of the Third Temple in Jerusalem. The tenth red heifer is believed to be prophetically significant as a requirement before the Third Temple can be consecrated.

Replacement theology—Also known as supersessionism. The belief that the church has replaced Israel in God's redemptive plan, rendering the Jewish people and their covenant obsolete. This view is challenged in Romans 11 and rejected by many Christian theologians.

Revelation 11:1–2—John is told to measure the temple, but exclude the outer court, which is given to the Gentiles. Seen by many as a hint that the Third Temple may coexist with Islamic holy sites on the Temple Mount.

Ritual cleanliness—A state required in the Old Testament to participate in religious ceremonies. Purification rituals like that of the red heifer restored ritual cleanliness after defilement (such as touching a dead body).

Ritually pure / ritual purity—The spiritual condition required to participate in temple worship and sacrifices. Ritual purity could be lost through normal life events (like death, disease, or bodily discharge) and had to be restored through God-prescribed purification practices.

Romans 11—A pivotal chapter in understanding God's continued plan for Israel. Paul warned against arrogance among Gentiles, assured that Israel's blindness is temporary, and promised a future restoration and salvation for Israel.

S

Seal/trumpet/bowl judgments—Three escalating sets of divine judgments in Revelation 6–16. Think of them as God pressing "increase intensity" in a world increasingly resistant to repentance. Like three stages in a movie trilogy, each one gets more intense than the last, moving the storyline toward the climax of Jesus' return.

Second coming of Christ—The prophesied return of Jesus to Earth as King and Judge. Many Christians believe it will be preceded by various signs, including tribulation, deception, and events like the rebuilding of the Jewish temple.

Second Temple / Zerubbabel's temple—Rebuilt by Jewish exiles after their return from Babylon (late sixth century BC), later renovated by Herod the Great. This was the temple active during Jesus' earthly ministry. Destroyed in AD 70 by the Romans.

Shimon the Just—A high priest during the Second Temple period, remembered in Jewish tradition for his righteousness and for overseeing some of the red heifer sacrifices.

Social media theology—A critique of modern Christian engagement that relies more on popular opinion and platforms than on Scripture for forming beliefs about Israel.

Solomon's temple—See "First Temple."

Spirit of the antichrist—Refers to a pervasive anti-Christ influence in the world that denies Christ and undermines truth (1 John 4:3). Separate from but related to the individual Antichrist.

Synagogue—A Jewish house of worship. In the New Testament, Paul often began his ministry in synagogues when entering a new city.

Syria Palestina—The new name given by Emperor Hadrian to Judea after the failed Jewish revolt in AD 135. This renaming was meant to sever the Jewish connection to the land.

T

Tabernacle / Tent of Meeting—A portable sanctuary built by the Israelites under Moses' leadership. It served as God's dwelling place before the temple was constructed. Its design was modeled after a heavenly pattern (Hebrews 8:5).

Temple desecration—The act of defiling the Jewish temple, historically by Antiochus Epiphanes, prophetically by the Antichrist (Daniel 9:27; 2 Thessalonians 2:4).

Temple Institute (Jerusalem)—An organization dedicated to preparing for the Third Temple, including training priests, recreating sacred vessels, and maintaining readiness for when the temple can be rebuilt.

Temple Mount—A sacred hill in Jerusalem considered the holiest site in Judaism and one of the holiest in Islam. Site of the First and Second Temples, the Dome of the Rock, and future Third Temple according to prophecy.

Temple worship—The system of sacrifices, prayers, festivals, and rituals carried out at the Jewish temples in Jerusalem. Participation in temple worship required ritual purity, which included purification through the red heifer.

Texas Red Angus ranch—A cattle ranch in Texas that reportedly became involved in the search for qualifying red heifers, visited by Israeli rabbis as part of a global search effort.

The Third Temple—A future temple in Jerusalem that many believe must be rebuilt for end times prophecy to unfold. Tied to the red heifer, sacrificial rituals, and the Antichrist's appearance in the Holy Place. Its construction is deeply controversial due to the presence of sacred Muslim sites on the same location.

"To the Jew first"—A phrase used by Paul (Romans 1:16; 2:9–10) indicating the priority of the Jewish people in God's redemptive plan. Not favoritism, but order. God first revealed Himself to them, and through them, brought salvation to the world.

Tribe of Dan—One of the twelve tribes of Israel, notably excluded from Revelation's list of the 144,000. Some early church fathers and scholars believed the Antichrist may come from this tribe.

Tribes of Judah, Benjamin, and Levi—The three tribes that primarily survived the Assyrian and Babylonian exiles. These formed the basis for the Jewish people during the time of Jesus and beyond.

Tribulation—A future seven-year period (based on Daniel 9) when God's judgment is poured out, evil rises, and many turn to Christ. The second half is often referred to as "the great tribulation."

Twelve tribes of Israel—The descendants of Jacob's twelve sons. These tribes formed the nation of Israel. After the division of the kingdoms, ten tribes were lost (see "Lost tribes of Israel").

Two witnesses—Two prophetic figures in Revelation 11 who preach, perform miracles, and are eventually killed and resurrected. Their identity is debated. Some say Moses and Elijah, others say symbolic figures.

Type and shadow—A biblical concept where an Old Testament person, object, or event symbolically represents a future reality fulfilled in the New Testament. For example, the red heifer is considered by some Christians to be a "type" of Christ—spotless, sacrificed, and used for cleansing.

U

Unblemished / without defect—Biblical language indicating that a sacrificial animal (like the red heifer) must be physically perfect, with no spots, marks, injuries, or prior use for labor. Symbolically, it represents purity and holiness.

W

Watchman—A biblical term for someone who warns others of coming danger (Ezekiel 33). In end times language, it often refers to someone paying attention to the signs and sounding the alarm. Used in chapter 7 as a call to readiness.

Y

Y2K—The year 2000 scare, which some interpreted as a potential apocalyptic event. Often cited alongside other failed doomsday predictions.

Yobel (Jubilee)—Hebrew word for "Jubilee," a fifty-year cycle outlined in Leviticus 25 involving trumpet blasts, restoration, freedom, and returning land. Tied to prophetic rhythms and the sound of Christ's return.

Yochanan / Yochanan the High Priest—A priest during the Second Temple era noted for preparing two of the nine red heifers, according to Jewish records.

Yoke—A wooden beam used to harness an animal for labor. For a red heifer to qualify for sacrifice, it must never have been yoked, symbolizing that it had not been used for any form of work or burden-bearing.

Yom Kippur—Known as the Day of Atonement, it is the holiest day in the Jewish calendar and central to themes of repentance and purification.

Z

Zerubbabel's temple—Another term for the Second Temple, originally constructed after the Babylonian exile, with political and spiritual opposition, later expanded by Herod the Great.

FREQUENTLY ASKED QUESTIONS ABOUT END TIMES AND BIBLICAL PROPHECY

General Questions

Q: What is eschatology and why should Christians care about it?

A: *Eschatology is the study of "last things" or end times, covering death, judgment, heaven, hell, Christ's return, resurrection, and humanity's final destiny. Christians should care because Jesus spent significant time teaching about His return, and understanding biblical prophecy helps us live with hope, urgency for evangelism, and proper eternal perspective.*

Q: What if I don't understand any of this?

A: *That's okay! The goal and hope of this book is to make these concepts approachable and digestible. Eschatology isn't just for scholars; it's for everyday believers trying to understand the times and be faithful in them.*

Q: Can we know when Jesus will return? Doesn't the Bible say we can't?

A: *Jesus said "no one knows the day or hour" (Matthew 24:36* NLT*). But Jesus and Paul also told us to be watchful and discerning of the season (1 Thessalonians 5:4–6). The goal isn't prediction, but preparation. We can't set dates, but we can be watchful and ready.*

Q: What's the difference between the rapture and the second coming?

A: *The rapture refers to believers being "caught up" to meet Jesus in the air (1 Thessalonians 4:17), while the second coming is Jesus physically returning to Earth to establish His kingdom. Different theological views place the rapture at different times relative to the tribulation period.*

Q: Why do Christians have different views on end times prophecy?

A: *The Bible uses symbolic language, metaphors, and imagery that can be interpreted differently. Major interpretive approaches include futurism (most prophecies are yet future), preterism (many fulfilled in AD 70), historicism (unfolding throughout church history), and idealism (symbolic of timeless spiritual truths). Regardless of a Christian's end times belief, it's secondary to salvation in Jesus Christ and Him alone.*

Q: Isn't focusing on end times prophecy a distraction from the gospel?

A: *While the gospel is central, biblical prophecy is part of God's Word and is meant to equip believers to live with hope, wisdom, and urgency (Titus 2:13; 2 Peter 3:11). Jesus Himself taught extensively about the end times (Matthew 24–25). He wants us to be prepared, not panicked. Living with a sense of urgency actually makes the gospel more important, not less.*

Q: What if Jesus doesn't return for a hundred years? Are we just wasting time?

A: *Not at all. Understanding biblical prophecy shapes how we live today, with urgency, wisdom, and a focus on the Great Commission. Whether Jesus comes tomorrow or one hundred years from now, we are called to live "ready."*

Q: Isn't all this just conspiracy theory wrapped in theology?

A: *It's easy to label unfamiliar or uncomfortable topics as conspiracy. But the red heifer, Temple Mount conflict, and temple preparation are all documented, visible, and historically rooted. The lens is biblical, not conspiratorial.*

Q: What about Muslims and the Dome of the Rock? Won't this spark a war?

A: *That's the tension. Any Jewish push to rebuild on the Temple Mount will likely provoke global backlash. Many believe this will be the spark that starts the fulfillment of end-time conflicts prophesied in Ezekiel and Revelation.*

Q: What does the Jewish Messiah have to do with Christians?

A: *For Christians, Jesus already fulfilled the messianic prophecies. But Orthodox Jews still wait for their messiah. Ironically, Scripture suggests the one they embrace may be the Antichrist—creating a chilling overlap in prophecy and deception (John 5:43; 2 Thessalonians 2).*

Red Heifer Questions

Q: What is the red heifer, and why does it matter in modern times?

A: *The red heifer, described in Numbers 19, was used for temple purification. It's the ceremonial reset button for Jewish temple worship. According to prophecy, its ashes are needed to purify a future temple, and that temple is part of the biblical domino effect leading to some major prophetic events. Many view the reappearance of qualified red heifers as the first step.*

Q: Isn't the red heifer just a coincidence or distraction? Why give it so much attention?

A: *While some dismiss it as religious sensationalism, the significance is rooted in both Jewish law and end-time prophecy. If Israel is actively preparing for the Third Temple, then the red heifer's presence is far from random. It's not just Reddit rabbit holes; literal headlines and ancient prophecies are colliding.*

Q: Doesn't the New Testament make temple sacrifices obsolete?

A: *Yes. Hebrews teaches that Jesus is the final and perfect sacrifice. However, from a prophetic standpoint, Scripture indicates the temple will be rebuilt and used again, most notably when the Antichrist defiles it (2 Thessalonians 2:4), not necessarily for God-honoring worship. For Christians, these temple sacrifices would be pointing to prophetic events, not necessary for salvation.*

Third Temple and Israel Questions

Q: Why is the Third Temple so controversial?

A: *Because its proposed site, the Temple Mount, is already home to the Dome of the Rock and Al-Aqsa Mosque, two of Islam's holiest sites. So if they start building, tension will rise quickly.*

Q: Are there real efforts happening now to rebuild the Jewish temple?

A: *Yes. Organizations like the Temple Institute have recreated garments, utensils, and blueprints in anticipation. The only missing piece is the perfect red heifer.*

Q: Has any temple ever stood on the Temple Mount in Jerusalem?

A: *Yes. The First Temple (Solomon's) and the Second Temple (rebuilt post-exile and later expanded by Herod) both stood on the Temple Mount. Many believe the Third Temple must be built on the same site.*

Q: If Jews rejected Jesus, how would God still fulfill prophecy through Israel?

A: *Paul addressed this in Romans 9–11, saying the Jewish people are still part of God's covenant and that "all Israel will be saved." And yeah, we can't imagine what that'll practically look like either. But Paul said their spiritual blindness is temporary, and their restoration plays a role in the timeline of Jesus' return.*

Q: Is modern Israel the same Israel from the Bible?

A: *This is heavily debated. Some believe modern Israel is a political nation unrelated to biblical prophecy; others see it as a fulfillment of Ezekiel 36–37. Some believe that prophecy concerning the land, the people, and the temple is indeed unfolding before our eyes.*

Q: Has the church replaced Israel in God's plan?

A: *This is called "replacement theology" or "supersessionism." Romans 9–11 suggests God's promises to Israel remain valid—that Gentiles are "grafted in" to God's covenant people rather than replacing Israel, and that God will yet fulfill His promises to the Jewish people.*

Antichrist Questions

Q: What or who is the Antichrist?

A: *Many biblical scholars believe the Antichrist will be a literal future world leader who opposes Christ and demands worship (2 Thessalonians 2; Revelation 13). However, Scripture also speaks of a "spirit of the antichrist" (1 John 4:3* NIV*) that operates throughout history, opposing Christ and truth.*

Q: What is the "mark of the beast," and will it be a physical mark?

A: *Revelation 13:16–17 describes a mark on the right hand or forehead required for buying and selling. Whether this is a literal physical mark, a symbolic representation of allegiance, or involves modern technology like digital IDs or implants is debated among scholars.*

Q: Why is Daniel's timeline important?

A: *Daniel 9 gives us the famous "seventy weeks" prophecy. Most scholars agree the first sixty-nine "weeks" (or sets of seven years) led up to Jesus' death. The seventieth week is where end-time watchers get the idea of a seven-year tribulation period. The theory is that we're in a prophetic pause, and when the clock resumes, things get apocalyptic.*

Rapture, Tribulation, and End Times Events

Q: When does the rapture happen? Before, during, or after the tribulation?

A: *Great question. And also one that has split Sunday schools since the 1800s. Some believe in a pre-trib rapture (we're out before it gets ugly), others a mid-trib (we're here for part of it), and some a post-trib (we're here for all of it and Jesus shows up at the end like a boss). There's also preterism, which believes many prophecies were fulfilled in AD 70. This is one of those "wrestle with Scripture and stay humble" topics.*

Q: What are the seal, trumpet, and bowl judgments?

A: *These are three escalating series of divine judgments described in Revelation 6–16, representing God's increasing intensity of judgment on a world resistant to repentance during the tribulation period.*

Practical Christian Living

Q: How should end times beliefs affect how I live today?

A: *Jesus emphasized readiness, faithfulness in our calling, love for others, and urgency in sharing the gospel. Whether Jesus returns today or in one hundred years, we should live holy lives, fulfill the Great Commission, and maintain an eternal perspective on temporary circumstances.*

Q: What if I'm wrong about my end times view?
A: *Eschatology involves secondary doctrines where faithful Christians often disagree. The essential is believing in Jesus' literal return and being ready. Whether you're pre-trib, post-trib, or amillennial matters far less than your relationship with Christ and obedience to His commands.*

Q: How do I respond to fear about end times events?
A: *Jesus said, "When these things begin to take place, stand up and lift up your heads, because your redemption is drawing near" (Luke 21:28* NIV*). For believers, end times events signal our hope's fulfillment, not cause for fear. God is sovereign, His plans will prevail, and believers have eternal security in Christ.*

Q: What about other religions' end times beliefs?
A: *Many religions have eschatological beliefs, but Christians believe the Bible provides the authoritative revelation of history's culmination. We can respectfully engage other views while maintaining confidence in biblical truth.*

Q: Where can I learn more or ask questions?
A: *A QR code has been provided at the end of the book for deeper resources, conversations, and community. You are not alone in this journey. God is unveiling His plan, and you're invited to watch it unfold with understanding and clarity.*

ACKNOWLEDGMENTS

To everyone who's been part of this *Faith and Friction* journey—you're the reason we wrote this book. Every download, DM, late-night question, and "wait, can we talk about this?" moment has reminded us that God is stirring a generation hungry for truth.

We've been blown away by the countless testimonies from people who've fallen in love with the Word of God again—people who once felt disillusioned, divided, or disconnected, but through honest conversation and healthy dialogue without judgment, have found themselves seeing Christ differently. That's the heartbeat of *Faith and Friction*: to create space for real questions that lead us closer to a real Savior.

To our families and friends who let us chase down every prophetic rabbit trail (and still showed up with coffee)—thank you for your love, patience, and prayers through every deep dive and deadline.

To our incredible team at W Publishing and our agent Tom Dean—thank you for believing in the vision, refining our voices, and helping us carry this message with excellence.

And to Jesus—the Author, the center, the soon-coming King—thank You for the grace to speak Your truth with courage and compassion. Every page, every word, and every ounce of friction is for Your glory.

Until You return, we'll keep asking the hard questions, wrestling through the tension, and helping people fall in love with Your Word all over again.

NOTES

Chapter 1

1. "Reaching the Nations," illumi*Nations*, accessed October 14, 2025, https://illuminations.bible/.
2. "And this gospel of the kingdom will be preached in all the world as a witness to all the nations, and then the end will come" (Matthew 24:14).
3. "The Tenth Red Heifer," Temple Institute, accessed December 10, 2025, https://templeinstitute.org/red-heifer-the-tenth-red-heifer/.

Chapter 2

1. Chris Livesay, "The Unlikely Role Red Cows Play in War Between Israel and Hamas," CBS News, March 2, 2024, video, https://www.cbsnews.com/video/the-unlikely-role-red-cows-play-in-war-between-israel-and-hamas/.
2. Livesay, "What These Red Cows from Texas Have to Do with War and Peace in the Middle East," CBS News, March 5, 2024, https://www.cbsnews.com/news/israel-war-hamas-red-heifers-from-texas-jerusalem-jewish-temple-al-aqsa/.
3. Mishnah Parah 3.5.
4. Mishneh Torah, Hilchot Parah Adumah 3:4.
5. Myles Hudson, "What Was Hadrian's Relationship with His Jewish Subjects?," *Britannica*, accessed December 11, 2025, https://www.britannica.com/story/what-was-hadrians-relationship-with-his-jewish-subjects.

Chapter 3

1. Edgar C. Whisenant, *88 Reasons Why the Rapture Will Be in 1988* (World Bible Society, 1988).
2. Yan Zhuang, "The Rapture Was Predicted to Happen Today. TikTok Has Some Advice," *New York Times*, September 23, 2025, https://www.nytimes.com/2025/09/23/us/rapture-tiktok-sept-23.html.
3. Jonathan Edwards, *The Works of Jonathan Edwards*, vol. 1, ed. Edward Hickman (Banner of Truth Trust, 1974), 11.
4. Livesay, "What These Red Cows from Texas Have to Do with War and Peace in the Middle East," CBS News, March 5, 2024, https://www.cbsnews.com/news/israel-war-hamas-red-heifers-from-texas-jerusalem-jewish-temple-al-aqsa/.
5. Shimon Eliyahu, "Did We Just Sacrifice a Red Heifer for Real?" *Messiah*, First Fruits of Zion, August 15, 2025, https://ffoz.org/messiah/articles/did-we-just-sacrifice-a-red-heifer-for-real.
6. Jason McKay and Annaly Mawire, hosts, *Faith and Friction*, podcast, "Byron Stinson Clears up the Rumors on the Red Heifer Sacrifice!", YouTube video, November 3, 2025, https://www.youtube.com/watch?v=YhpaZ0uRiAw.

Chapter 4

1. Jared T. Parker, "Cutting Covenants," in *The Gospel of Jesus Christ in the Old Testament*, ed. D. Kelly Ogden et. al. (Religious Studies Center, Brigham Young University, 2009).
2. Orit Avnery, "How Did the Word 'Jew' Become Identified with the Jewish People?," Shalom Hartman Institute, January 22, 2011, https://www.hartman.org.il/how-did-the-word-jew-become-identified-with-the-jewish-people; "Chapter One -- Are the So-called 'Lost' Tribes of Israel Really Lost?" in *America & Britain* (Church of the Great Commission), https://www.cbcg.org/booklets/america-britain/chapter-one-are-the-so-called-lost-tribes-of-israel-really-lost.html; Philip Neal, "Are the So-Called 'Lost' Tribes of Israel Really Lost?," chap. 1 in *America &*

Britain (York Publishing Company, 2014), https://www.cbcg.org/images/books/America-and-Great-Britain.pdf.

Chapter 5

1. John Piper, "To the Jew First, and Also to the Greek," sermon, Desiring God, July 5, 1998, https://www.desiringgod.org/messages/to-the-jew-first-and-also-to-the-greek.
2. *Faith and Friction*, podcast, season 2, episode 10, "Cosmic Warfare," June 17, 2024, YouTube video, 1:04:56, https://www.youtube.com/watch?v=35A-3PJ_jjM.
3. "Dramatic Decrease of Israel Supporters Among Young Evangelicals," Tel Aviv University, February 12, 2024, https://english.tau.ac.il/news/declining-support-of-young-evangelicals.

Chapter 6

1. Vendyl Jones, *A Door of Hope: My Search for the Treasures of the Copper Scroll* (Lightcatcher Books, 2005).
2. Shelley Neese, "Interview with Jim Barfield about The Copper Scroll Project," *The Jerusalem Connection Report*, January 1, 2009, https://thejerusalemconnection.us/interview-with-jim-barfield-about-the-copper-scroll-project/; "Transcipt of Tamar Yonah's Interview of Copper Scroll Project Director Jim Barfield," The (Retired) Blog of Robert R. Cargill, Ph.D., August 24, 2009, https://bobcargill.wordpress.com/2009/08/24/transcript-of-tamar-yonahs-interview-of-copper-scroll-project-director-jim-barfield/.
3. "The Tenth Red Heifer," Temple Institute, accessed November 4, 2025, https://templeinstitute.org/red-heifer-the-tenth-red-heifer/.
4. Dr. Robert Mawire, personal conversation with Annaly Mawire, February 20, 2024.
5. Don Stewart, *The Jews, Jerusalem, and the Coming Temple: Center Stage for the Final Countdown* (pub. by author, 2020), https://cdn.subsplash.com/documents/4F3F27/_source/5c135d89-42f2-4e73-ae63-de0ff7bdf152/document.pdf.

6. Christian Widener, *The Temple Revealed: The True Location of the Jewish Temple Hidden in Plain Sight* (End Times Berean, 2020).
7. Widener, *The Temple Revealed.*

Chapter 7

1. The White House, "US President Trump's Proclamation on Jerusalem as the Capital of the State of Israel," United Nations, December 6, 2017, https://www.un.org/unispal/document/us-president-trumps-proclamation-on-jerusalem-as-the-capital-of-the-state-of-israel/.
2. Adam Eliyahu Berkowitz, "Netanyahu Compares Trump to Cyrus in Compliment of Biblical Proportions," *Israel365News*, March 6, 2018, https://israel365news.com/322196/?utm_source.
3. "Trump-Cyrus Half-Shekel Temple Coin," Temple Coins, accessed December 15, 2025, https://www.temple-coins.com/products/half-shekel-cyrus-trump-temple-coin.
4. US Department of State, "The Abraham Accords," 2017–2021 archived content, accessed November 5, 2025, https://2017-2021.state.gov/the-abraham-accords/.
5. Abraham Accords Peace Agreement: Treaty of Peace, Diplomatic Relations and Full Normalization Between the United Arab Emirates and the State of Israel, U.A.E.-Isr., Sept. 15, 2020, U.N.T.S. No. 56565, https://treaties.un.org/doc/Publication/UNTS/No%20Volume/56565/Part/I-56565-08000002805a7d1f.pdf.
6. Pinhas Inbari and Dan Diker, "The Temple Mount Status Quo: An Anchor of Stability in a Sea of Regional Radicalism," Jerusalem Center for Security and Foreign Affairs, October 1, 2024, https://jcpa.org/the-temple-mount-status-quo-an-anchor-of-stability-in-a-sea-of-regional-radicalism.
7. Inbari and Diker, "The Temple Mount Status Quo."
8. Inbari and Diker, "The Temple Mount Status Quo."
9. Inbari and Diker, "The Temple Mount Status Quo."

10. Boneh Israel, accessed December 16, 2025, https://www.bonehisrael.com/.
11. David Rosenthal, "Red Heifers and the Fight for Al-Aqsa," Zion's Hope, February 5, 2025, https://zionshope.org/blog/2025/02/05/red-heifers-and-the-fight-for-al-aqsa.
12. "Fulfillment of Prophecy Anticipated: Unblemished Red Heifers for Temple Coming of Age," *Charisma*, May 22, 2023, https://charismanews.com/news/world/fulfillment-of-prophecy-anticipated-unblemished-red-heifers-for-temple-coming-of-age/.
13. Dr. Robert Mawire, personal conversation with Annaly Mawire, February 20, 2024.
14. Martin Sieff, "Embattled Israel: Why Netanyahu Lost," UPI, December 5, 2002, https://www.upi.com/Defense-News/2002/12/05/Embattled-Israel-Why-Netanyahu-lost/80221039116015/.
15. Mawire, personal conversation.

Chapter 8

1. *Strong's Exhaustive Concordance of the Bible*, under "*shâbûwa* (H7620)," accessed October 19, 2025, https://www.blueletterbible.org/lexicon/h7620/kjv/tr/0–1/.
2. Harold W. Hoehner, *Chronological Aspects of the Life of Christ* (Zondervan, 1977), 126.
3. Robert Anderson, "The Prophetic Year," chap. 6 in *The Coming Prince*, (Pickering & Inglis, 1900); Charles F. Redeker, *The Biblical Prophetic Year: Its Length, Origin and Application* (Tract Publications, 1983), https://www.biblechronology.org/studies/biblical_prophetic_year.pdf.
4. Biblical Archaeology Society Staff, "Herod's Death, Jesus' Birth and a Lunar Eclipse," Biblical Archaeology Society, December 22, 2024, https://www.biblicalarchaeology.org/daily/people-cultures-in-the-bible/jesus-historical-jesus/herods-death-jesus-birth-and-a-lunar-eclipse/.
5. Yoma 39b, accessed July 18, 2025.

Chapter 9

1. Richard M. Davidson, "The Bible and Hermeneutics: Interpreting Scripture According to the Scriptures," in *Christ in the Classroom: Adventist Approaches to the Integration of Faith and Learning*, vol. 31B, ed. Humberto M. Rasi (Institute for Christian Teaching, Education Department, General Conference of Seventh-Day Adventists, 2004), 81–132, https://christintheclassroom.org/vol_31B/31Bcc_081-132.htm?utm_source.
2. John Calvin, *Institutes of the Christian Religion*, trans. Henry Beveridge (Hendrickson, 2008) 4.7.25.
3. Tacitus, *The Annals of Imperial Rome*, trans. Michael Grant (Penguin Classics, 1996), 411 (15.44).
4. E. W. Bullinger, *Number in Scripture: Its Supernatural Design and Spiritual Significance* (1894), 282–287.
5. *Britannica*, "Nero," last modified June 19, 2025, https://www.britannica.com/biography/Nero-Roman-emperor.
6. 1 Maccabees 1:10–64; 2 Maccabees 6:1–17; Josephus, *Antiquities of the Jews*, trans. William Whiston (Project Gutenberg, 2024), bk. 12, chap. 7–9.

Chapter 10

1. *Faith and Friction*, podcast, season 1, episode 2, "Artificial Intelligence," YouTube, August 14, 2023, https://www.youtube.com/watch?v=WjqBBI9jWAk&list=PLOJNtdC1L3Ax2WGpE-Hs8YhCR4jai33Oz&index=3.
2. C.E. Hill, "Antichrist from the Tribe of Dan," *Journal of Theological Studies* 46, no. 1, (April 1995): Gale Literature Resource Center.
3. Hippolytus, *Treatise on Christ and Antichrist*, in *Ante-Nicene Fathers*, vol. 5, ed. Alexander Roberts and James Donaldson (Eerdmans, 1989).
4. Annaly Mawire et al., hosts, *Faith and Friction*, podcast, season 1, episode 4, "Nephilim, Who Are They?," YouTube, 34:04,

September 11, 2023, https://www.youtube.com/watch?v=JgKAYsG-NPI; *Faith and Friction*, podcast, season 2, episode 6, "Nephilim, Demons, and Fallen Angels," April 22, 2024, YouTube, 52:33, https://www.youtube.com/watch?v=vvdWROr7boU.

5. "Nephilim," EBSCO, accessed October 20, 2025, https://www.ebsco.com/research-starters/religion-and-philosophy/nephilim.
6. George Noory, host, "Nephilim Secrets," *Coast to Coast AM*, June 11, 2013, radio broadcast, https://www.coasttocoastam.com/show/2013-06-11-show/.

Chapter 11

1. *Strong's Exhaustive Concordance of the Bible* (1890), under "hemera (G2250)," accessed December 16, 2025, https://www.blueletterbible.org/lexicon/g2250/kjv/tr/0-1/; *Strong's*, under "hora (G5610)," accessed December 16, 2025, https://www.blueletterbible.org/lexicon/g5610/kjv/tr/0-1/.
2. *Strong's*, under "chronos (G5550)," accessed December 16, 2025, https://www.blueletterbible.org/lexicon/g5550/kjv/tr/0-1/; Strong's, under "kairos (G2540)," accessed December 16, 2025, https://www.blueletterbible.org/lexicon/g2540/kjv/tr/0-1/.

Chapter 12

1. *Strong's*, under "harpazō (G726)," accessed December 16, 2025, https://www.blueletterbible.org/lexicon/g726/kjv/tr/0-1/.
2. "Jerome Completes the Vulgate," *Christian History 28* (1990), https://christianhistoryinstitute.org/magazine/article/jerome-completes-vulgate.
3. Cyrus I. Scofield, ed. *The New Scofield Reference Bible: New American Standard Bible* (Oxford University Press, 1967), note on 1 Thessalonians 4:16–17.
4. J. D. King, "Exposing The Rapture Myth You've Been Taught All Your Life," (blog), updated December 20, 2024,

https://www.jdking.net/post/exposing-the-rapture-myth-you-ve-been-taught-all-your-life.

5. Gustav Adolf Deissmann, *Light from the Ancient East: The New Testament Illustrated by Recently Discovered Texts of the Graeco-Roman World*, trans. Lionel R. M. Strachan (George H. Doran Company, 1927), 372.
6. *The New Strong's Exhaustive Concordance of the Bible*, "apantēsis (G529)," accessed December 16, 2025, https://www.blueletterbible.org/lexicon/g529/kjv/tr/0-1/.
7. David Guzik, "Ezekiel 38: The Defeat of Gog and Defense of Israel," Enduring Word Bible Commentary, accessed November 6, 2025, https://enduringword.com/bible-commentary/ezekiel-38/.

ABOUT THE AUTHORS

Annaly Mawire, Jason McKay, and Chichi and Tracy Onyekanne are the voices behind *Faith and Friction*, a podcast that quickly found a global audience after its launch in 2023. *Faith and Friction* seeks to confront the challenging conversations that cause friction in the church. This space for honest, sometimes uncomfortable, conversations resonates with a community of listeners eager for thoughtful, scripture-centered discussions on the tensions within the church. Together, they navigate these complex conversations with a spirit of humility, truth, and curiosity, always pointing their audience back to the Word of God and a deeper, personal relationship with the Holy Spirit.

LET'S GO DEEPER

We know there's a lot to unpack when it comes to prophecy and the end times—so we created extra resources to help you keep exploring.

Scan the QR code to access:

The Holy Cow Study Guide—Whether you're reading solo or gathering with friends, this guide walks you through every chapter with discussion questions, reflection prompts, and action steps. Perfect for individual study or small groups!

***Faith and Friction* podcast episodes**—Hear extended conversations and insights that didn't make it into the book.

And don't forget to check out the **Glossary and FAQ sections** in the back of this book—it's your quick-reference guide for all things end times, from key terms to common questions believers are asking today.

Because this journey isn't about having every answer, it's about discovering the truth together, one conversation at a time.